WHITE LIES

Race, Class, Gender,
and Sexuality in
White Supremacist Discourse

WHITE LIES

Race, Class, Gender,
and Sexuality in
White Supremacist Discourse

Jessie Daniels

Routledge
New York & London

Published in 1997 by
Routledge
29 West 35th Street
New York, NY 10001

Published in Great Britain by
Routledge
11 New Fetter Lane
London EC4P 4EE

Library of Congress Cataloging-in-Publication Data

Daniels, Jessie, 1961–
    White lies : race, class, gender and sexuality in white
supremacist discourse / by Jessie Daniels.
        p.   cm.
    Includes bibliographical references and index.
    ISBN 0–415–91289–X (alk. paper). — ISBN 0–415–91290–3 (pbk. :
alk. paper)
    1. White supremacy movements—United States. 2. United States—
Race relations. 3. United States—Social conditions—1980–
4. Discourse analysis—Social aspects—United States. I. Title.
E184.A1D245 1996
305.8′00973—dc20
                                              96–21014
                                                 CIP

For three from whom I have learned so much—

Patricia Hill Collins
Joe R. Feagin
Christine L. Williams

Contents

List of Illustrations

Preface

On Epistemology, Whiteness, and Sexual Politics: Personal Reflections on Standpoint and White Supremacist Discourse

"The sociological imagination," C. Wright Mills wrote, "is the intersection of biography and history" (1959). Over the last two decades, feminist scholars in a variety of fields have proven the truth of this insight, and taken it to dimensions Mills could not have envisioned (and probably would not have embraced), by arguing for the importance of the personal in understanding the political.

Standpoint, as so many feminist scholars have noted, is important to epistemology and to the theory we develop; claims to "objectivity" are but obfuscations of stance whether acknowledged or not. The analysis of white supremacist discourse which follows here has been influenced by my standpoint; and, at the same time, my understanding of that standpoint has been influenced by my analysis of white supremacist discourse.

During the course of doing research for this book, I learned that my paternal grandfather was, for a brief period of time, a member of the Ku Klux Klan in Texas during the 1920s. In the time that has passed since discovering this, I have pondered how to come to terms with this information in the context of this book. The debate I was having with myself involved whether or not I should publicly "disclose" that he had been a Klan member. On the one hand, this fact constituted part of my standpoint. On the other hand, his membership was very brief (the story goes that he joined because he found the idea of being part of a "moral crusade" appealing, but dropped out when he saw that the group was intent on racial violence), and remains an unpleasant, and little discussed, artifact of my family history. There were no Klan robes that were handed down as part of a family legacy, and I discovered the fact of his membership quite by accident. Furthermore, by exposing this obscure detail of personal history, I would certainly risk being dismissed by critics as either a white liberal, consumed by guilt, trying to atone for the sins of my grandfather; or, worse still, I would somehow be labeled an apologist for white supremacist ideology, which I most definitely am not. My experience has been that many people assume that a white person doing research on white supremacists must be sympathetic to their cause. So, it seemed this fact was better left out. It was not that relevant, after all, and revealing this seemed an act of disloyalty to my family. I finally decided, however, that the "disloyalty" was not to my family, it was to "whiteness." As Mab Segrest puts it, "The white supremacists had it right, in some ways, I was in fact, a 'race traitor,' disloyal to the cause of whiteness" (1994).

But there was another, more difficult issue that I grappled with about telling this family secret. If I were to reveal that my grandfather was a Klan member, should I go on to reveal that he was the very same grandfather that molested me as a child? I think not. Surely, this is much too personal, and not relevant. But the debate continued in my mind, and I wondered why I considered it relevant to reveal one and not the other. And, further, doesn't this perfectly illustrate my point about race, gender, and sexuality being intertwined? I then realized the importance of including this narrative here. The further irony is that this Klan member and child-molester raised *my* father, who was most certainly not abusive and who, for his generation, held astonishingly egalitarian views of gender. He, along with my mother, raised me—a girlchild born in the early 60s of Texas, where "feminism" was a dirty word—to believe unreservedly in myself and in my abilities, to believe that I could be or do anything. And yet, my gender-egalitarian father could simultaneously harbor and espouse ideas about, even argue enthusiastically for, Black inferiority and Jewish corruption. It was not until many years later that I understood that, in large measure, the belief in my ability that pervaded my girlhood was predicated on being white and middle-class. It was based on the conviction that I would grow up to occupy that space of complete agency and privilege that my maternal grandmother referred to as being "free, white, and twenty-one."

Part of the privilege of my girlhood was that I was considered at a relatively young age (10, 11, 12) a full, intelligent human being; and, at that age, I enjoyed, almost more than anything, debating ideas with my father into the wee hours of the night. As he would attest, I began disagreeing with my father about racial politics (and doing so vehemently) early on.

For reasons that are still not clear to me (perhaps I sensed that I could somehow be excluded with such thinking; perhaps I had absorbed the cultural messages from outside my home about the civil rights movement; perhaps I identified with my oldest brother, eleven years my senior and a bona fide, long-haired, hippie radical; perhaps I just wanted to disagree with my father), I argued against his views, primarily of Black inferiority. Those late-night discussions gave me special insights into white supremacist thinking; after all, I grew up trying to think and argue against it.

My standpoint has influenced my analysis of epistemology, whiteness, and sexual politics, and my analysis has influenced how I view my standpoint. Thus, my personal experience of privilege (being white and middle-class) and oppression (being a woman and a lesbian) has given me a particular angle of vision for analyzing white supremacist discourse and has also deeply affected me. It has made me more aware of my own position as a "subject" or target (as a "race traitor") of white supremacist attacks (whether symbolic or physical), and the ways that subject position is connected to others. My analysis has also made me even more aware of my own privilege, and how this, too, is predicated on the complicated nexus of race, class, gender, and sexuality.

In the course of writing this book, after spending hours reading white supremacist literature, I would have (and continue to have) nightmares. In these night visions, I transgress boundaries of class, gender, and sexuality. In one dream it is nighttime and I am covered with sweat, exhausted from running, and hiding in a ditch; the sweat is pouring down into my eyes. My heart is pounding so loudly I am sure it will give me away. And then, from the cover of the ditch I am in, I see them, the men who are after me. They are night-riders, men on horseback in white hoods, illumined like specters by the torches they carry. I know that if these white men come upon me—the Black man they are hunting—if they catch me, they will torture me, castrate me, burn me alive, then hang my body from a tree on the courthouse lawn. I wake with a start and wonder if I escaped.

In another dream, I am sitting on a park bench in Brooklyn, crying hot tears of anger, talking to a Black woman whom I soon realize is my grandmother. She is telling me that it won't do me any good to live with the consequences. My feeling sorry for myself won't make it any better, so I should just hush my crying. I tell her that I'm not crying because I'm feeling sorry for myself; I'm crying because I'm angry. Angry because I've just come from the Upper East Side where I've seen a white women, pregnant like me, encircled by her white friends. As I walk by them, I see that they are laughing, talking, giving her gifts—a baby shower, perhaps? I smile with recognition, anticipation at the joy of a new life, but then that smile goes away as these white women turn to look at me—young, Black, and obviously pregnant—their eyes filled with hatred, anger, disgust. "Why can't those people learn to control themselves?" one says. Another says, "Tsk, tsk, such a pity." And finally, "What a waste." I am back on the park bench, talking to my grandmother again, telling her that I'm angry because I know the world will welcome that white woman's baby and not mine.

And, in yet another dream, I have just come out to my class as a lesbian, and the students rise from their chairs, approaching me at the lectern. As they approach, I realize that they have all brought baseball bats with them to class (perhaps because they had their suspicions about me?) and they begin to pummel me with their bats.

For me, this kind of terrorism exists primarily at the level of the subconscious. But this awareness of being the "subject" of white supremacist discourse has given me, as much as anything else, an even deeper realization of my own privilege within a white supremacist context. Through the course of my daily life, I do not encounter racial hostility or overt threats of homophobic violence or more than the usual amount of gender oppression; instead, I can often coast on the privileges of middle-class whiteness and the presumption of heterosexuality.

Acknowledgments

This book would not have been possible without the remarkable people at Klanwatch, the division of the Southern Poverty Law Center which monitors (and often successfully puts out of business) extremist white supremacist organizations. My thanks to Morris Dees for founding the Center and Klanwatch; to Danny Welch, director of Klanwatch, for access to their archives; and to Joe Roy, head of research, for sharing his wealth of knowledge about contemporary white supremacist organizations.

This books draws on research I completed for my doctoral dissertation, and the members of that committee—Joe R. Feagin, Lester Kurtz, Desley Deacon, Doug Kellner, Dale McLemore, and Christine Williams—lent the weight of their substantial individual and collective wisdom to this project and challenged me to make the work better. Susan E. Marshall and Sheldon Ekland-Olson also contributed to the project in its earliest stages. The University of Texas at Austin provided financial support through the last years of graduate school. Joe Feagin and Christine Williams deserve more of my gratitude than the space here allows me to express; this is why I have dedicated this book to them.

Jana Walters and Dana Britton spent many more hours coding, analyzing, discussing, and thinking about white supremacist discourse than they ever intended, and for that I owe them both my thanks. I particularly want to thank Jana Walters for listening patiently to my early attempts at articulating connections between extremist and mainstream white supremacy and for encouraging me to "bridge the gaps."

The Charles Phelps Taft Fund at the University of Cincinnati generously provided me with a Taft Postdoctoral Fellowship that allowed me the luxury of time to read, write, research, and think more about white supremacy. I particularly want to thank Joanna Mitro for making it happen, even on a picket line, and the Departments of Sociology and African American Studies, especially Ms. Sadie Oliver. The students in my seminar, "Exploring White Racism," read an earlier draft of this book and offered me their insightful comments on it. Kerry Welch, at RAPP, remains a valuable ally and fellow "race traitor." I would never have been a Taft Postdoctoral Fellow if it had not been for the largess and generosity of Pat Hill Collins, for which I am deeply grateful. Pat Collins gave me more in my brief stay in Cincinnati than a few words in an acknowledgment can address; this is why this book is also dedicated to her.

While at Florida Atlantic University, Mary Rivers Cure, Linda Perez McDonald, and Marcela Tribble proved to be exceptional students and insightful reviewers of my work. Marcela Tribble also contributed much assistance with a variety of research and administrative tasks. The College of Liberal Arts provided institutional support with computer facilities, copies, and office supplies.

Kevin Harper and Martha Adams, along with Gary and Ellise Knowls, gave me a place to come home to, time to relax, and the space to be myself, and they loved me no matter what. They are simply the best. And I want to thank their children, Daniel, Deborah Anne, Lorne, Jennifer, Brian, and Kyle, for connecting me to the next generation and for reminding me of what is important.

I want to thank Nancy Bell and Deb Siegler for their house and their friendship, which provided me a space of refuge and support, and a space for imagining new realities. It was in their house, on one of those timeless Austin afternoons, that I first thought of this project.

I owe a special debt of gratitude to Kate Adams for introducing me to the writings of Dorothy Allison, Minnie Bruce Pratt, and Mab Segrest and to the journal *Race Traitor*, and for reminding me of Lillian Smith's work. I cannot emphasize enough how important these works have been in shaping my thinking. And I continue to be grateful for and rely on Kate's unflinching willingness to engage in discussions, often for hours at a time, about the privileges of whiteness and about the particular mix of privilege and oppression involved in being a white lesbian. These conversations have sustained me and renewed my energy at a number of critical points.

My editors at Routledge, Jayne Fargnoli and Anne Sanow, believed in this project early on and provided just the right combination of encouragement and constructive criticism. Their efforts have made my writing, and this book, better; and I thank them for that.

1

Introduction

A good deal of time and intelligence has been invested in the exposure of racism and the horrific results on its objects . . . that well-established study should be joined with another, equally important one: the impact of racism on those who perpetuate it. . . . The scholarship that looks into the mind, imagination, and behavior of slaves is valuable. But equally valuable is a serious intellectual effort to see what racial ideology does to the mind, imagination, and behavior of masters.

—*Toni Morrison,* Playing in the Dark, *1992*

This book is an investigation into the white supremacist imagination. I explore here the *terra incognita* of publications produced by extremist white supremacist organizations in the contemporary United States, and what I find is disturbing.

An illustration of a white man shows him standing before towering skyscrapers and bridges while an airplane flies overhead; the caption reads, "White Men *Built* this Nation, White Men *Are* this Nation!" In another drawing, a buxom white woman stands bare-breasted, holding a machine gun, and casts a seductive glance at the viewer; the caption reads, "Get a White Man and Screw the System." A caricatured drawing of a Black man—complete with exaggeratedly large lips, protruding eyes, bulging crotch, and a gun—is labeled "Today's Young Coon." In another drawing an obviously pregnant Black woman—again, caricatured with huge lips and protruding eyes—stands dazed from smoking what appears to be a crack pipe, while in her hand she holds several government

1

checks; three anonymous, white, male hands offer her other forms of government assistance. The caption here reads, "There's a Lot of Talk These Days about Civil Rights . . . But *Never* a Word about *Civil Wrongs!*" A Jewish man, denoted by his large nose and the Star of David symbol on his tie, appears menacingly in another drawing; beneath him, the caption reads, "The Evil Jew." And a woman who is signified as Jewish (again by her excessively large nose) and as lesbian (by the two-women symbol tattooed on her arm) represents the "Jew-dyke-feminist conspiracy" that turns "women into dykes."

These horrifying images provide a quick glimpse of what is conjured up by the white supremacist imagination in the publications of contemporary white supremacist organizations in the United States. What is most alarming about the white supremacist discourse produced by extremists is that it shares much in common with the white supremacist discourse produced by elected officials, Madison Avenue, mainstream political debate, academic intellectuals, and popular culture representations. In this book I analyze the ways this discourse is situated within the particular racial and class context of institutionalized white supremacy. I also examine the ways certain notions of gender and sexuality are woven into white supremacist discourse. My argument here is that central to the "white lies" on which white supremacist discourse rests is the construction of "whiteness"; and that white supremacist discourse legitimates and sustains privileges of race, class, gender, and sexuality that are inherent in a white supremacist context.

Extremist white supremacist discourse, and the people and organizations that produce that discourse, represent for most of us an unexplored region of kooks, cranks, and crazies ranting about race with a zeal that clearly marks them as the extremists they are, far removed from everyday life or encounters. Most of us do not know anyone personally who is, or would even consider being, a member of one of these organizations. Recently, most Americans have become acquainted with white supremacists through films, news reports and a variety of popular books, or through their frequent appearances on talk shows such as "Geraldo," "Donahue," "Oprah," and "Sally." Who are these people who call themselves "white supremacists," "white separatists," or simply those who "stand up for white rights"?

White supremacists are "true believers," in Eric Hoffer's sense of that term. White supremacist organizations attract people who are seeking a refuge from the "anxieties, barrenness and meaninglessness of an individual experience" (Hoffer, 1951). As Ben Klassen, founder and former leader of the Church of the Creator, one of the organizations examined here, noted about his followers, "They're activist young people who know some-

2

thing's wrong but they don't know what to do about it. They encounter the Church of the Creator and find the answer." Yet this explanation for the existence and increasing growth of white supremacist organizations is not very satisfying. Such an analysis could just as easily apply to people in fundamentalist religions, whether Christian, Islamic, or Jewish, or those in religions otherwise known as "cults," or those zealously committed to a host of other extremist causes. As Lipset, and Raab (1970) have pointed out, extremism is a part of American culture. Yet the argument that white supremacists are "just part of the extremism" that is endemic to United States society tends to "e-race" the very specific manifestation of white supremacist organizations and their discourse, and does not tell us anything about their connection to the broader context of racial politics.

Any endeavor to analyze the discourse of white supremacist organizations can be hindered by an impulse to dismiss the organizations, or their discourse, as irrelevant. Questions often arise which reflect this, such as: How seriously should we take white supremacists? Are they a real threat, or are they part of a lunatic fringe that, if simply ignored, will go away? Or, alternatively, are they part of a lunatic fringe that will always exist? These questions seem to be shaped by a white paradigm in which the study of "race" has meant an almost exclusive focus on the purported pathology of people of color. Asking whether or not white supremacists are a real threat misses the point that white supremacist discourse has very real consequences for people of color. However, the question of how seriously we should take white supremacists must also be addressed here. Although the focus of this book is explicitly on the *discourse* of white supremacist organizations, rather than on why or how individual people come to appropriate that discourse and or join white supremacist organizations, arguments which assert that white supremacists are only a distant threat tend to undermine any serious analysis of this discourse.

The argument I want to address, then, is this: White supremacists constitute a very small number of people and therefore are not a threat. Out of over two hundred and fifty million people in the United States, only about 40,000 are white supremacists, less than 1 percent of the population. In addition, those white supremacists represent an extreme fringe of racist sentiment that does not reflect the sentiment of most Americans. Public opinion polls consistently show that Americans are becoming more tolerant with regard to race.

Furthermore, white supremacist organizations are full of individuals who are marginal members of society. They tend to be unemployed and/or poor, uneducated, and probably mentally unbalanced. Given the context of a faltering economy, these people are easily duped into seeing white supremacist organizations as an answer to their own economic distress. Once the economy improves, then white supremacists, and their organizations, will disappear.

The marginal individuals who are attracted to white supremacy are most often Southerners. White supremacy is an affliction of one, especially racist, region of the country, the South. White supremacist organizations do not have nationwide appeal, and therefore, white supremacy is not a national issue, it is a regional one.

Finally, white supremacist organizations represent a vestige of an older, more racist era. Eventually, white supremacists will simply fade from the American landscape. Like dinosaurs, they will become extinct. More importantly, white supremacist rallies are often more heavily attended by protesters than supporters, sometimes by ratios of 10 to 1. Clearly, white supremacists are not a real, widespread threat if this is the kind of response that greets them.

Though these may seem to be compelling arguments, they have some serious flaws. Let me consider each of these arguments in turn. First, while it is true that white supremacists constitute less than 1 percent of the population, let me suggest that what you consider a "small enough" number to *not* constitute a threat has a great deal to do with positionality. If you are among the vast majority of the white population that is not a member of a white supremacist organization, such organizations may simply represent for you an annoyance, or perhaps an offense to your sensibilities of what is good and just. Thus, the 1 percent of white supremacists may seem an insignificant, if unfortunate, statistic. If, however, you are a person of color, and you are a *target* of white supremacists and their discourse, then white supremacists may represent a material threat to your life. Thus, the thought of 40,000 avowed white supremacists means that there are that many more threats in the world that you must deal with.

And it is worth noting that estimates of the numbers of white supremacists are notoriously imprecise. White supremacists often give media sources numbers which are too high to boost their visibility, and those who wish to minimize the impact of white supremacists often underestimate their numbers. Still, the most reliable information available suggests that the "small numbers" (depending on where you're standing) of white supremacists are growing steadily. Klanwatch, an organization which monitors white supremacist activities in the United States, estimates that there were 362 white supremacist organizations here in 1992, an increase of just over 27 percent from the previous year. In addition, the lessons of history teach us that relatively small numbers can grow astronomically in astonishingly short periods of time.

While it is true that surveys consistently show a trend over time toward increasing attitudes of "racial tolerance," public opinion polls also show that a majority of white Americans agree with many of the basic ideas white supremacists espouse. In fact, according to the 1991 General Social Survey, 78 percent of whites thought Blacks were more likely than whites to prefer living on welfare, and 74 percent thought Hispanics more likely to prefer welfare. In the same study, 62 percent of whites thought Blacks were less likely to be hard-working; 56 percent thought Blacks were more prone to violence; 53 percent of whites thought Blacks were less intelligent; and 51 percent thought them less patriotic (*New York Times,* January 10, 1991, B10).

The notion that white supremacists are poor or unemployed, uneducated, and mentally unbalanced is a persistent one. It is also a comforting notion somehow to think that those who advocate the glaring racism examined here are set apart from those of us who are not poor, or those who are at least gainfully employed, educated, and relatively stable mentally. Unfortunately, this is no more than a comforting fiction. Studies which compare members of white supremacist organizations to the general population reveal that, in terms of aggregate statistics, members do not differ significantly from the population as a whole on measures of income, education, and occupation. Of the leaders in the white supremacist organizations represented in this study, five out of eight hold college degrees and two hold advanced degrees (see chapter 2).

The relationship between white supremacist organizations and the economy is a complex one and remains less than entirely clear. While it is possible that an increase in white supremacist organizations may be related to economic decline, it is certainly not a causal relationship. Indeed, the most popular resurgence of the Ku Klux Klan occurred during an era of unprecedented economic prosperity, the 1920s. Moreover, this explanation relies on a facile class-race model, which is no longer feasible given more complex understandings of race and class.

White supremacist organizations, while at one time a predominately Southern phenomenon, are no longer restricted to a particular region of the country. In fact, white supremacy is a regionally diverse, national movement.

With every incarnation—from the Reconstruction Era of the 1860s, to the 1920s resurrection, to the present manifestation—white supremacist organizations have been reported to be dying out, the last vestige of a bygone era. What seems clear, however, is that rather than a momentary aberration (or a recurring nightmare)' white supremacist groups are an entrenched feature of United States racial politics. The persistence of white supremacist organizations may be a testament to Derrick Bell's assessment of the "permanence of racism" in American culture (1992).

And, finally, while it is true that white supremacists are often outnumbered at their own rallies 10 to 1 by counter-demonstrators, the sad irony is that these protests themselves often turn violent. It is difficult to think of a more tragically misdirected or ineffective strategy than, as frequently happens at such rallies, to resort to violent attacks against white supremacists because "they hate people."

More importantly in terms of response to white supremacist organizations, government leaders at the highest levels have been virtually silent on this issue. The United States government has pursued white supremacist organizations for "sedition," but not for racism. In addition, white supremacist discourse is protected under the aegis of the First Amendment. These two strategies, on the one hand pursuing white supremacists for "sedition," but not for racism, and taking a protective stance in favor of their speech on the other hand, combine to institutionalize white supremacy, tacitly approving its message.

Perhaps more to the point, whites are not, by and large, organizing to dismantle institutionalized white supremacy or to combat white supremacist discourse in arenas outside extremist groups, or white supremacist ideology, on an ongoing basis. Instead, anti-Klan demonstrations are typically conducted on an *ad hoc*, sporadic basis in response to specific actions by white supremacists.

Given this context, there has traditionally been little space available for "seeing race" at all in white supremacist movements. Analyses which lump white supremacists into the category "extremists" miss the otherwise self-evident point that white supremacist organizations and their discourse are first and foremost "about" race. For people whose lives may depend on what actions individuals take based on white supremacist discourse, there is little doubt that they are to be taken dead seriously.

Throughout this book, I point out the ways that the ideologies of the white supremacist movement are connected to more mainstream representations of white supremacy; and further, how these are related to notions of gender and sexuality. I will now lay out in preliminary fashion my argument about white supremacist organizations and their discourse.

Theoretical Origins

In this book, I make three main theoretical arguments. First, I contend that central to the "white lies" on which white supremacist discourse rests is the construction of "whiteness." The construction of "whiteness" linked to the social, historical, and ongoing political process responsible for the ascendancy of "race"; and the mechanisms of this process become clearly

6

visible in efforts within the discourse to construct "whiteness," "Blackness," and "Jewishness" as essential identities.

Second, I contend that it is impossible to examine the construction of race without simultaneously interrogating class, gender, and sexuality. This suggests that in terms of understanding theoretical linkages between race, class, gender, and sexuality, instead of conceptualizing these as separate or discrete categories, we need to look at the process of creating these divisions as a singular one.

Third, I demonstrate that the themes of race, class, gender, and sexuality that appear in extremist white supremacist discourse resonate effectively in mainstream politics, advertising, academia, and popular culture. I further assert that white supremacist discourse—whether produced by extremists, Madison Avenue, or academics—serves to sustain privileges of race, class, gender, and sexuality which are endemic to a white supremacist context. In the following section, I briefly trace the theoretical antecedents which led me to these assertions.

My primary theoretical interest is research with white supremacy and the connections to class, gender, and sexuality. So, rather than beginning with an interest in white supremacist groups *per se* (which may have led me to a more sociologically conventional avenue of investigating of the groups as "deviants" or as one of many types of "extremist" social movements), my own intellectual path, given my previous research on lynching, led me to view white supremacist organizations and their discourse as connected to a context of institutionalized white supremacy.

A key development in recent scholarship theorizing race is the racial formation approach, which highlights contemporary political contestation over racial meanings. From this perspective:

> there is no unitary racial ideology in the United States, but there are a number of competing political projects which seek to articulate a particular understanding of race and its meaning for social and political life. (Omi, 1990:2–3)

The implication here is that the idea of "race," rather than being a biological certainty, is a socially and politically constructed category. Furthermore, Omi's reference to the "competing political projects" attempting to "articulate a particular understanding of race" suggests that forging and maintaining distinct racial categorizations requires elaborate ideological work.

"Race," from this perspective, "is understood as an unstable and 'decentered' complex of social meanings constantly being transformed by political struggle" (Omi & Winant, 1986:68). Recognizing this makes it all

7

the more necessary to understand particular instances in which "race" has become a meaningful social category (Gilroy, 1987:38). The racial formation approach suggests that racial meanings, or the meanings of "race," are sites of struggle, are "contested terrain" (Hall, 1986:5–27).

Omi and Winant employ this perspective to explain the effectiveness of challenges from the far right to ideals of racial equality promoted by social movements of the 1960s. They contend that economic arguments are inadequate for understanding the development of the far right, which includes the white supremacist movement. Instead, the growth of far right political movements, such as the white supremacist movement, represents:

> a political response to the liberal state and reflects a crisis of identity engendered by the 1960s. The far right attempts to develop a new white identity, to reassert the very meaning of *whiteness*, which has been rendered unstable and unclear by the minority challenges of the 1960s. (Omi & Winant, 1986:116)

Here, Omi and Winant offer an illuminating way of understanding contemporary racist ideologies. The efficacy of racial discourse as articulated by white supremacist groups is shown to be a response to challenges to white hegemony in the 1960s which successfully contested the value of, indeed, the very notion of "whiteness." This ability to reassert the meaning of "whiteness" is what Omi and Winant refer to when they point out the right's ability to "*rearticulate* the meaning of race in contemporary American society" [emphasis mine] (Omi & Winant, 1986:113). It is this process of rearticulation, of reasserting the very meaning of "whiteness," which is central to racist ideologies and to the white supremacist project.

Parameters

The study of white supremacy and "whiteness" is receiving an increasing amount of attention by scholars, journalists, and activists. I want to contribute to our emerging understanding of the peculiar social and historical construction of whiteness. And, I want to focus particular attention on the way gender, sexuality, and class are implicated in this process. It is also my intention to develop strategies for combatting extremist white supremacist organizations, such as the ones examined here. The book is not, however, intended to be an exhaustive study of the contemporary white supremacist movement. This study is also not meant to "broadcast" white supremacist ideas. Such an approach is an ineffective and poten-

8

tially damaging strategy for battling white supremacy. Legal scholar Mari Matsuda sets out the argument in this way:

> ". . . the 'fresh-air' position . . . suggests that the most effective way to control the Klan is to allow it to broadcast its ideas. When people are exposed to the hatred propagated by the Klan, they will reject the Klan and organize against it. Suppressing the Klan will only force it to choose more violent and clandestine means of obtaining its goals. (Matsuda, 1933:33)

My strategy is not, as in the "fresh-air" position, to "air" or broadcast white supremacist ideas so that people will be exposed to them and therefore reject them. I do not think this is an effective mechanism for combatting the white supremacist movement or its discourse. As Matsuda convincingly argues, such speech *acts on* people of color and has a material and deleterious impact. And, for white listeners (or readers), any resistance which might have been prompted by broadcasting white supremacist ideas is often subverted: instead of being mobilized into action against white supremacist organizations, white people may be persuaded in favor of white supremacy or even subtly inured to its impact. Broadcasting may also serve to comfortably distance the majority of white people from those who proudly claim to be racists, and thus from any interrogation of their own position within a broader white supremacist context.

Rather than merely "airing" white supremacist views, my aim is to provide a critical framework for analyzing white supremacist discourse. Readers will then begin to see the barrenness of these "white lies"—whether in extremist publications or the evening news—and begin to recognize their own position within a broader context of white supremacy.

In this chapter, I have set out some of the theoretical issues which are relevant to this project. In the following chapters, I bring together these themes and examine them further. In chapter 2, I look at the way white supremacist movements exist within a white supremacist context. That is, I explore the social, political, and historical context shaped by capitalism that privileges whiteness as a social category and simultaneously privileges maleness and some forms of heterosexuality. Also in chapter 2, I provide an overview of white supremacist movements in the United States, as well as a look at specific groups and publications. In chapter 3, I examine the publications themselves and probe the construction of "whiteness" within the discourse. Whiteness is actively constructed within these publications along lines of gender and sexuality. In chapter 4, I turn to the images of African Americans in the discourse. I demonstrate here, too, that in the white supremacist imagination, the racial Other is constructed not only as

9

racial beings but also as gendered and sexualized beings. In chapter 5, I look at the ways Jews are imagined by white supremacists and the great pains to which white supremacists must go to construct Jews as "non-white," the possession of "white skin" being a necessary, but not sufficient, criterion. In each of these chapters, I demonstrate the ways that these extremist images are cruder versions of images which pervade more mainstream political discourse and popular culture. In chapter 6, I look at what the mapping of white supremacist discourse can tell us for theorizing race, class, gender, and sexuality. I also contemplate the implications of the persistence of avowed white supremacist organizations at the end of the twentieth century in the United States and briefly examine some of the political implications of such an analysis.

tying W.S. to mainstream

White Supremacist Movement(s) in a White Supremacist Context

America became white—the people who, as they claim, "settled" the country became white—because of the necessity of denying the Black presence and justifying the Black subjugation.

—*James Baldwin, "On Being White and Other Lies," 1984*

White supremacy in the United States is a central organizing principle of social life rather than merely an isolated social movement. My aim in this chapter is to place the analysis of white supremacist movements and their discourse within a broader context of white supremacy as a social system. I also will provide an account of the historical development of white supremacy as institutionalized privilege and as ideological justification for such a practice. The place to begin such an account is with the big lie, the "white" lie, that makes all the other lies of white supremacist discourse possible.

"On Being White": A History of the Lie

"Race," as an idea, is relatively new on the cultural horizon. Prior to the sixteenth century (not that long ago in historical terms), the concept of "race" was unheard of; and until the middle of the nineteenth century (a mere heartbeat, historically speaking), the term was not commonly used. Surely, one might argue, physical differences between peoples have long been recognized, and indeed, they have been. Images of people with dark skin, broad noses, thick lips, and tightly coiled or wooly hair, what some have referred to as the "Negroid" phenotype, appear in Egyptian art as early as the latter part of the third millennium B.C. (Snowden, 1990:5). However, the ancient world did not emphasize "color"—or what we today think of as "race"—as a significant human distinction. People whom we would today classify as racially "Black" (such as Ethiopians) associated freely—socially, culturally, and intimately—with those we would, through a twentieth-century American lens, consider "white" (such as Greeks and Romans). Indeed, the "Black" culture of Ethiopia was held in high esteem by Mediterranean people. And, while people certainly viewed their own cultures in ethnocentric terms (Greeks, for example, referred to many other cultures as "barbarian"), these assessments were not based on biological notions of "race," nor were they linked to (perceived) physical characteristics or traits. (For a much more thorough treatment of the world before "race," see the fascinating work of St. Clair Drake and Frank Snowden.)

Perhaps the earliest appearance of something like the idea of "race" emerged in 1095, when Pope Urban II preached a sermon urging his followers to reclaim their Holy Land from Moslems, or "infidels." The Moslems were not close at hand, but the Jews were, and within six months after the Pope's sermon, the Jews at Worms were massacred by Christian Crusaders (Gossett, 1963:10). This ignominious point marks the beginning of contemporary anti-Semitism and has undeniable parallels to contemporary notions of "race" and its seemingly inevitable attendant, racism.

The idea that a social identity like "Jewishness" was linked to inheritable characteristics first emerged within the Christian imagination about the Jews. Jews were believed by some Christians to be despicable creatures with a host of inferior physical, mental, and moral qualities. These traits were presumed to be "hereditary," as well, since the Jews invariably "passed on" all of these negative attributes to their children. In the litany of Christian beliefs about Jews in the middle ages, we can see the foreshadowing of contemporary racism: Jews were thought to have an unpleasant odor; they were thought to carry diseases, especially in the blood, that Christians did not. Gender and sexuality figured in these early images as well: a Jewish man's beard reportedly resembled that of a goat, known at that time to be a "lecherous" beast; simultaneously, Jewish men were believed to menstruate (Gossett, 1963:11).

The sixteenth and seventeenth centuries brought with them the dawn of the colonial era. Europeans set out to circumnavigate the globe in search of natural resources for their respective monarchies. And it was in this context that colonialists began to encounter new peoples and the idea of "race" began its ascendancy. By the sixteenth century, debate raged throughout Spain and the rest of Europe about the ontological status of the indigenous peoples encountered in the "new world" (the "Indians"): were they human, beast, or some other, hitherto undiscovered, intermediate being? And, it was in 1619 when a writer, reading accounts of colonial travelers, was inspired to speculate that Ethiopians (the same people whose culture had been widely admired and whose phenotype was little remarked on a few centuries prior) must be closely related to apes because of their darker skin color and must have once walked on all fours (Gossett, 1963:15).

As James Baldwin suggests in the epigraph to this chapter, the invention of the "white race," was an effective means of denying the Black presence and simultaneously justifying their oppression. Emergence of the term "white" as a meaningful category was tied to the development of an economic system of racial slavery, after the subjugation of Blacks became a firmly entrenched practice (Allen, 1994).

For Native Americans, early debates about their ontological status as human, beast, or intermediate had been settled by concluding that they were definitely "not white," but debate still continued about whether or not Native Americans could be "converted" to Christianity (a sure indication of their status as human beings if they could be). While missionaries, and many other Christians, decided that they were human beings, and hence, eligible for conversion, the rest of the country remained undecided. The United States government's policy toward these "non-white" peoples remained one of genocide through a variety of means. At the time of the European conquest of North America, there was an estimated population of 15 million Native Americans which declined to 250,000 by 1890 largely because of firearms and European diseases (Thornton, 1987).

"White Power": Institutionalized White Supremacy in the Economy

More than half a century after W. E. B. Du Bois observed the twentieth-century problem of the "color line" (1939), we remain, as Andrew Hacker has so compellingly demonstrated, a racially divided nation, separate, hostile, and unequal (1992). White supremacy is built into the fabric of our society so that being "white" is a systematic advantage, especially economically. "Whiteness" as a racial category is predicated on economic inequality as a key feature and mechanism in the perpetuation of the color line which separates us into two nations.

Economic power in the United States is highly concentrated in the hands of a few, and overwhelmingly in the hands of whites. Indeed, Dye (1983) estimates that only about 4,300 individuals—or two one-thousandths of 1 percent of the population—exercise formal authority over the largest proportion of the nation's assets. Of these 4,300, the overwhelming majority are white, male, and from the upper class or upper middle class.

Obviously, the vast majority of white Americans do not hold this kind of power or have access to this amount of wealth. Still, the average white families' wealth ($39,135) is almost ten times that of the average Black family ($3,397); and a full 30 percent of Black families have no wealth or negative net worth because of debts, while the same is true for only 8.4 percent of white families (Feagin & Feagin, 1993:235). The median income for white families was approximately $36,000 compared to only $21,000 for Black families in 1990. This contrast in earnings becomes even more stark when we break those figures out by gender, with white men having a median income of $21,000, almost double that of $12,000 for Black men; for white women, the median income is a mere $10,000, still more than the barely $8,000 median for Black women (Hacker, 1992:94). The fact remains that for those white Americans, both men and women, who must struggle to survive in the absence of class privilege, their economic prospects are still much better than those of Black men and women.

Although racial discrimination in housing has been officially illegal for more than twenty years, residential segregation remains a prominent feature of American life. White Americans prefer, overwhelmingly, to live in all-white or mostly white settings. Surveys that reveal that an increasing majority of whites say that it would "be okay" if a Black person moved into the neighborhood, or even next door, are often heralded as evidence of the declining significance of race. But study after study shows that white people vote with their moving vans, and a presence of about 7 percent of minorities will have whites calling their real estate agents and looking for a new residence. The result is what some scholars have referred to as an American version of apartheid. White children "grow up white" in all-white settings and attend schools that are predominately white.

[handwritten margin note: residential segregation]

A Brief History of the White Supremacist Movement in the United States.

White supremacist movements may seem superfluous in a white power structure. After all, in a society which so privileges "whiteness" at every turn and in which whites still control the overwhelming majority of the wealth, power, and prestigious positions, what function is served by the presence of such extremist groups espousing blatantly racist ideology? More precisely, who benefits from the existence of such groups? These are questions to which I will return, but first, it is important to set out the historical context in which white supremacist groups have emerged.

The most notable group within the white supremacist movement in the United States has been the Ku Klux Klan. The Klan has appeared in several incarnations: the Reconstruction-era Klan; the Klan of the 1920s; the civil rights-era Klan; and the contemporary Klan, which represents only one part of the current white supremacist movement.

The original Klan was founded in the late 1860s as an all-male social club in Pulaski, Tennessee, for Civil War veterans of the former Confederate states. Initially dubbed "the Pulaski Circle," the group eventually changed its name, choosing "Ku Klux" as a slightly altered version of the Greek word for circle, *kuklos*. Later, "Klan" was added for alliterative purposes (Lester, 1905:21). The Ku Klux Klan was quickly transformed from a social to a political organization, committed to maintaining the racial hegemony of whites in the face of Reconstruction. Members terrorized blacks with night rides (robed Klansmen on horseback carrying torches) and lynchings. But the Reconstruction Klan soon withered as whites found other means to relieve their boredom and began to feel more sure of their dominant racial position as Reconstruction gave way to the assurance of white hegemony through the institutionalization of Jim Crow segregation. After the Klan's fall, a revisionist history surrounding its role in saving the South from the perils of Reconstruction was widely believed. Prevailing mythology held that the original Klan:

> proved a great blessing to the entire South and did what the State and Federal officials could not do—it brought order out of chaos and peace and happiness to our beloved South. (Lester & Wilson, 1905:21)

This interpretation of the Klan's historical function would later play a role in its resurgence and prove that reports of the death of the Ku Klux Klan had been greatly exaggerated.

The Klan reemerged in the 1920s and reached new heights in terms of membership and mainstream respectability. From an estimated membership of 5,000 in 1920, the Klan claimed over five million members in 1925 from a wide variety of regions across the United States.[1] The organization was guided by William J. Simmons. Simmons originally conceived of the Klan as a fraternal order, much like the Masons, Elks, and other such organizations experiencing widespread popularity during this time. Simmons was, depending on the account, an entrepreneur or huckster who envisioned the Klan not only as an opportunity for white, Protestant men to associate fraternally, but also as an endeavor for which membership fees could make him a wealthy man (Clawson, 1986).

The organization, officially begun in 1915, floundered for the first several years. The release of D. W. Griffith's film that same year, *Birth of a Nation,* an adaptation of Thomas Dixon's novel, *The Clansman,* which told the revisionist history of Reconstruction, provided just the inspiration Simmons needed to transform his fledgling order. This early film was hugely popular and was even shown at the White House to an appreciative President Woodrow Wilson. The film, like the book, drew on the widely accepted view of the Reconstruction-era Klan as the savior of the South from a host of evils including powerful, menacing Blacks who held political office, along with Northern carpetbaggers and scalawags. In addition to saving the Southland, the Klan was pictured as guarding "pure, white, Southern womanhood" against those who would ravage it. In the film, Klansmen are seen lighting crosses (which the first Klan never actually did). Simmons adopted the burning cross as a symbol for a Klan meeting atop Georgia's Stone Mountain and set the tone for the dramatic decade to follow. Simmons also provided a permanent symbol for the Klan. The "fiery cross" is still a staple of Klan iconography. Klan members contend that they "light," rather than "burn," crosses in order to "illuminate the principles of Jesus Christ" (Wade, 1987).

In the 1920s the Ku Klux Klan was enormously popular among white Protestant Americans, both men and women. In fact, a sociologist writing at the time declared the Klan to be "the most spectacular of all the social movements in American society since the close of the World War" (Medklin, 1924:3). Klan-supported candidates won local and statewide elections, and one Klan candidate was nearly elected president.

Klan membership at this time was regionally diverse with some of its strongest chapters located outside the South. Blee's study, for example, examines the case of Indiana, while Moore studies the Klan in Colorado, Indiana, and Orange County, California. This research indicates that on every available measure Klan members were not marginal to the mainstream of society, but were instead pillars of their communities. Membership of the 1920s Klan was representative of the general population on variables such as income, education, and occupation. And, unlike the earlier organization, this Klan was not an exclusively male preserve. Indeed, an estimated 500,000 women joined the Women of the Ku Klux Klan (WKKK), the women's auxiliary of the Klan. In some states, women comprised nearly half of the membership of the Klan and represented a significant minority in others (Blee, 1991:2).

There has been much debate in sociological research about why the Klan was so immensely popular at this point in history. Traditional explanations for the Klan's resurgence during the 1920s have emphasized factors such as the migration of Blacks from the South to the North, residual nationalistic hatred of immigrants and political "radicals" fueled by World War I propaganda, and a general increase in bigotry and intolerance directed at ethnic groups concentrated in urban areas by white Protestants in rural areas, as well as a rise in religious and political fundamentalism. All of this occurred within a context of rapid social change and great geographic mobility in which the Klan positioned itself as the guardian of law and order and traditional values. Customary interpretations of this social upheaval describe the national embrace of the Klan as a retreat from the Progressive Era, part of the "politics of despair" of far-right extremism (Chalmers, 1987; Lipset & Raab, 1970).

More recently, however, scholars have taken issue with this traditional explanation for the dramatic emergence of the Klan in the 1920s. Moore, for example, argues that ethnic conflict was *not* a basis for the rise of the Klan, but that the organization instead drew on discontent rooted in broader social change and the "erosion of traditional values" (Moore, 1991:185). Moore also finds that the Klan was concentrated in both urban and rural areas where white Protestants represented an overwhelming majority and the Klan enhanced a sense of "white Protestant ethnic identity" (Moore, 1991:187). Recent work has also argued that the Klan, rather than representing a retreat from the political reforms of the Progressive Era, was emblematic of a desire to carry on many of the goals and ideals of the Progressive era, rather than a desire to abandon them (Moore, 1991).

Some critics have rejected the conventional split between "progressive" and "reactionary" movements because this bifurcation is not useful in understanding why the ideology of the Klan was so appealing to large numbers of women. For Klanswomen of the 1920s, there were varying, often contradictory ideologies underlying their commitment to the goals of the organization. Women of the KKK, as Blee has noted:

> carried into their struggle against Blacks, Jews, Catholics, labor radicals, socialists, Mormons, and immigrants a belief in gender equality among white Protestants in politics, work and wages. (Blee, 1991:59)

Blee goes on to argue that the mobilization of women into the 1920s Klan linked racist sentiments like those that motivated men to join the KKK, to a "specific gendered notion of the preservation of family life and women's

17

rights" (Blee, 1991:67). The reality of women's suffrage was that rather than unifying a block of female voters around what suffrage advocates characterized as "essentially feminine" issues such as peace, divisions of race became more salient for white, Protestant women.

Still other factors which contributed to the Klan's growth included the network of lodges, Protestant churches, and clubs which structured life for many whites in 1920s America. The Klan drew on this network and gained much of its strength from it. In addition, the regionally specific nature of Klan campaigns allowed for much of its growth. For example, local Klaverns could target Blacks in Southern regions, Catholics in the Northeast, and Mormons in Utah (Blee, 1991).

The popularity of this embodiment of the Klan began to wane as the twenties wore on. By 1927, Klan membership had fallen to approximately 350,000. Scandals involving top Klan leadership began to surface in 1926, and these were responsible for much of the disillusionment and attendant fall in membership, but these scandals alone cannot fully explain the Klan's fall from prominence at the end of the twenties. The collapse of the Klan is generally attributed to "economic depression, internal battles, and financial scandals" (Blee, 1991, p. 72). The decline has also been attributed to elections won in the late 1920s by members of the KKK which:

> affirmed that . . . [the] white Protestant majority was still in command. Men and women who had believed that the foundation of their way of life might be crumbling beneath their feet could feel an uncommon sense of satisfaction. Deeply held traditional values, a common ethnic bond, and a sense of community seemed to have been upheld. (Moore, 1991:185)

White, Protestant hegemony had been reaffirmed in many respects by the end of the decade and so, in a sense, the Klan was a victim of both cooptation and its own successes. At the end of the 1920s, few agreed on what was responsible for the rise and fall of the KKK, though most agreed that the Klan was dead and would not be resurrected.

Although never completely defunct, the next widespread revival of Klan activity began when the organization mounted a violent attack against the civil rights movement of the 1960s. Estimates are that roughly 65,000 people were official members of the Klan in 1965. The Klan was directly linked to a profusion of violence targeted at Blacks during the 1960s, including the assault on freedom riders and the bombing of a church in which four young Black girls were killed. As the civil rights era faded, the Klan declined once more. In 1974, Klan membership reached a twentieth-century nadir of 1,500.

The Contemporary White Supremacist Movement

Since the early 1970s, total membership in white supremacist organizations has increased annually. By 1978, Klan membership was up to approximately 9,000 members; by 1981 the Klan could claim roughly 11,000 members. Since 1981, however, membership in the Klan has fallen to roughly 5,000. In fact, by the early 1980s, the Klan was in decline as other, more radical white supremacists began to ridicule it openly, deriding the robes and hoods, the elaborate alliterative nomenclature of klaverns, kleagles, and klatches, and the march-and-protest strategy that characterizes the group (Stanton, 1991:253). Although the Klan appears to be on the decline, the white supremacist movement is not.

In the past two decades, the Klan has been joined by a plethora of other organizations espousing racist ideology such as the Posse Comitatus, Christian Identity, White Aryan Resistance, Neo-Nazi Skinheads, and Creativity. While there are important ideological differences between these groups (which I will address), they all share a commitment to maintaining white racial hegemony (Langer, 1990).

Membership in these new branches of the white supremacist movement has exploded. While accurate estimates of membership in white supremacist organizations are difficult to obtain, the most conservative estimates place the combined membership in white supremacist organizations at around 40,000 dues-paying members and growing (Flynn & Gerhardt, 1989; Klanwatch, 1992; Langer, 1990; Smothers, 1991; Zatarain, 1991).

Although the precise number of members of the white supremacist movement is often impossible to ascertain, tracking white supremacist organizations is somewhat easier. In 1991, the number of white supremacist groups in the United States grew to 346, up from 273 in 1990, an increase of 27 percent (Klanwatch, 1992). White supremacist groups are eager to grow and thus seek out, and benefit from, media attention (Calbreath, 1981; Harper, 1993). In addition, white supremacist organizations frequently publish newsletters or newspapers (such as the ones examined here) to further their cause, and this makes them easier to identify.

The diversification of the white supremacist movement over the last twenty years has meant a division in movement activity between an aboveboard political movement led by David Duke and an underground movement that is armed and increasingly violent. In 1989, David Duke, the former Grand Wizard of the KKK, won a seat in the Louisiana legislature; in the fall of 1990 he came remarkably close to pulling off an upset when he drew 44 percent of the vote against incumbent Senator J. Bennett Johnston in the general election. In 1991, Duke garnered 55 percent of the white vote in a statewide election for governor of Louisiana. And in Arkansas, a leader of the Christian Identity branch of the white supremacist movement had a substantial showing in the 1990 race for the Republican nomination for lieutenant governor (Stanton, 1991: 254).

One of the more disturbing aspects of the contemporary white supremacist movement is the development of new and extremely violent branches of the movement including organizations such as the Skinheads and Creators (members of the Church of the Creator). These groups threaten to become the foremost white supremacist groups in the country. The rise of these white supremacist organizations has had deadly consequences for many racial and ethnic group members. One estimate is that between 1986 and 1991 "at least half a dozen racially or ethnically motivated murders committed by Skinheads have been reported in states stretching from Oregon to Florida" (Stanton, 1991:254). In March 1981 in Mobile, Alabama, a young black man, Michael Donald, was murdered by Klan members. After he was killed, his body was hung "lynch style" from the branch of a tree on the courthouse lawn. In November 1988 in Portland, Oregon, an Ethiopian refugee was clubbed to death by three Skinheads. In July 1993, eight white supremacists were arrested and charged with plotting to kill Rodney King, bomb Los Angeles' First African Methodist Episcopalian Church, and send a bomb to a rabbi all in an effort to start a racial war. Those arrested are reported to be Skinheads and Creators (Applebome, 1993). While it should be stated that not all hate crimes are committed by members of white supremacist groups, and not all members of white supremacist groups participate in violence, there is a clear and well-documented connection between members of these groups and racial violence.

Membership in the contemporary white supremacist movement is regionally diverse. Available research on the contemporary white supremacist movement (Aho, 1990), like studies on the Klan of the 1920s (Blee, 1991; Moore, 1991), reveals that members of white supremacist organizations do not differ significantly from the general United States population in education, occupation, or income. While previous studies point to an inverse relationship between racism and variables such as years of education and socioeconomic status (e.g., Lipset & Raab, 1970), more recent research convincingly challenges these contentions. Aho, for example, finds that among Christian Patriots in Idaho, members were just as well, if not *better*, educated than the general population of Idaho. In addition, Aho finds that with regard to occupational distribution, Christian Patriots do not differ significantly from the general population of Idaho. Finally, in terms of income, members of the white supremacist group fared about the same as Idaho residents in general (Aho, 1990).

To date, scholarly treatment of white supremacist groups has focused almost exclusively on the Klan (Alexander, 1965; Blee, 1991; Chalmers, 1987; Katz, 1986; Lipset & Raab, 1970; Mecklin, 1924; Moore, 1991). A great deal of the extant writing on white supremacist movements is in a journalistic vein (Flynn & Gerhardt, 1989; Langer, 1990; Sims, 1970; Ridgeway, 1990; Wade, 1987; Thompson, 1982). This concentration is understandable given the prominence of the Klan over the last century. Most of this research shares an interest in the organizations' history and its membership. Specifically, the majority of scholars who study these organizations seek to understand what kind of people join and why they join (Omi's work is the only exception here). While these are important, indeed invaluable, insights, it is also necessary to place white supremacist movements within a broader social context. Such a shift in focus brings into view the way these organizations and their discourse function to sustain hierarchies of race, class, gender, and sexuality.

White Supremacist Movements in a White Supremacist Context

There is some scholarship which is beginning to cast white supremacist discourse and organizations within a broader political context. In their discussion of white supremacists, Omi and Winant (1986) suggest that white supremacists are connected to other efforts on the new right and the far right to "rearticulate whiteness," that is, to reclaim "whiteness" as a positive and affirming identity after the challenges of the 1960s and 1970s called the very existence of "whiteness" into question. They suggest that white supremacists may serve as "shock troops" for the far right (Omi & Winant, 1986:118). In a later article, Omi contends that the inclination to dismiss white supremacist groups as "extremists," and therefore not worthy of serious attention, elides the more important point that, "throughout the history of the U.S., the 'extremism' of the far right has often converged with the cultural and political center" (1991:85).

Likewise, Feagin and Vera (1994) convincingly argue that white supremacist groups are only one form, albeit an extreme one, of a phenomena that pervades contemporary United States society—white racism. And, in a similar vein, James Ridgeway writes that the white supremacist discourse "remain[s] disconcertingly close to mainstream politics" (1990:8). Perhaps most persuasive in this argument are legal scholars Matsuda, Lawrence, Delgado, and Crenshaw, in their co-authored volume, *Words that Wound* (1993). Each of the authors, in turn, makes a compelling case for the place of white supremacist discourse—what they refer to as "hate speech"—as part of a system of institutionalized white su-

21

premacy. Lawrence makes the point that racist speech and discriminatory conduct are inseparable because they are both part of a white supremacist totality. He goes on to state that:

> The goal of white supremacy is not achieved by individual acts or even by the cumulative acts of a group, but rather it is achieved by the institutionalization of white supremacy within our culture has created conduct on the societal level that is greater than the sum of individual racist acts. (1993:61)

Lawrence's assessment is an astute one; white supremacist discourse and institutionalized white supremacy are linked. The linkage is not so much that words incite action (though this does clearly happen). Rather, the connection is that institutions and discourse—from a variety of mechanisms and at a range of sites—operate concurrently to privilege the lie of "whiteness."

In placing white supremacist movements and their discourse within a broader context, I want to return to questions I raised earlier about the functions these groups serve and who benefits from their existence. To paraphrase and restate Hartmann—all men benefit from patriarchy, and some men benefit more than others (1985). I contend that all whites benefit from white supremacy, and some whites benefit more than others, and that the presence of extremist groups works to sustain white supremacy as an ideological justification for institutionalized privilege. To the extent that they confirm the social order as it exists, that is, they affirm institutionalized white supremacy.

How, one may legitimately ask, do all whites benefit from such overt expressions of racism? Here, we can turn to Delgado:

> I believe that racist speech benefits powerful white-dominated institutions. The highly educated, refined persons who operate . . . universities [and] major corporations would never, ever themselves utter a racial slur. That is the last thing they would do. Yet, they benefit, and on a subconscious level they know they benefit, from a certain amount of low-grade racism in the environment. If an occasional bigot or redneck calls one of us a nigger or a spick one night late as we're on our way home from the library, that is all to the good. . . . This kind of behavior keeps non-white people on edge, a little off balance. We get these occasional reminders that we are different, and not really wanted. It prevents us from digging in too strongly, starting to think we could really belong here. It makes us a little introspective, a little unsure of ourselves; at the right low-

grade level it prevents us from organizing on behalf of more important things. It assures that those of us of real spirit, real pride, just plain leave—all of which is quite a substantial benefit for the institution. (1993:82)

Delgado is referring to the grinding toll extracted by dealing with racial humiliation on a daily basis. The extra energy it takes to cope with the continual barrage of indignities, even among those who have achieved middle-class standing, is well-documented (Feagin & Sikes, 1994). In addition, the continued presence of white supremacist organizations, producing volumes of white supremacist discourse, day after day, month after month, year after year, under the legal protection of the United States government, and simultaneously dismissed as "insignificant" by the vast majority of white citizens, adds to the debilitating effect of living under a system of white supremacy for people of color.

In many ways, the presence of white supremacist organizations and their discourse functions to confirm the social order for whites in much the same fashion that, in another historical context, lynching—violence directed primarily at Black men—functioned. Even those not implicated, those who may have been appalled by such "vulgar" displays, still reaped the rewards of living in a system in which being born white was a social condition vastly privileged over being born Black. That white supremacists periodically act on these beliefs only confirms what many people of color already know about life in a white supremacist context—their lives are in danger.

And, while I recognize the problematics of reasoning by analogy to other forms of oppression, there are some parallels between, for example, anti-Semitic acts and pogroms that serve to reinforce a Christian-dominated world and rape, which, as a form of male terrorism, effectively controls women and serves to reinforce a male-dominated society as well as gay-bashing which silences lesbians and gay men as it affirms a heteronormative order. So, too, violent actions and the symbolic violence of white supremacist discourse affirms the white power structure. Herein lies one of the chief problems of trying to understand oppression through analogy: lived experience seldom fits neatly within one side of the analogy. White supremacist discourse accomplishes all of these functions at once. It is not that white supremacist discourse is "about race" and they "hate women too" (though this is certainly true at some level); it is that within the white supremacist imagination—as it is expressed in extremist movement discourse, or as it is institutionalized—race, class, gender, and sexuality are woven together in complex, and mutually reinforcing ways.

In many respects, the prevailing view among academics and the general public that white supremacist organizations are merely "fringe" groups, and hence, not worthy of serious attention, serves important functions for reinforcing systems of privilege. Within sociology, this trend has been most evident in the sub-disciplinary specialities which have taken up the study of white supremacist organizations: social movements and deviance. (See, for example, Lipset & Raab, 1970, for perhaps the best example of this; and also Perlmutter & Perlmutter, 1972. The notable exception to this trend in sociology is Blee, 1991. For deviance, see Hamm, 1993, and the work of Levin & McDermott, 1992.) While the scholarship here is certainly first-rate and provides us with valuable insights into the organizations, I want to suggest that examinations of white supremacist organizations and their discourse from either a social movements or a deviance analytical framework makes it difficult to conceptualize these groups as connected to a larger (white supremacist) context. For example, if white supremacist movements are studied along with other "extremist" groups, this tends to highlight aspects considered "extreme" and diminishes the significance of race. Likewise, if such groups are studied along with other "deviants," attention is then focused on the ways in which white supremacists are different from, rather than similar to, the rest of Americans. By obfuscating the connections between white supremacist movements and the white supremacist context in which they exist, traditional paradigms "e-race" the central importance of being "white." And, more to the point, these interpretations leave unexamined—indeed, completely irrelevant within such a framework—the privileged position of white academics, or the ways white supremacy (with all the connections to class, gender, and sexuality in place), are inscribed in academic institutions.

This view is reflected outside the realm of academic scholarship, as well. In a different milieu, nationally syndicated shows—such as "Donahue," "Geraldo," "Oprah," and "Sally"—offer an important lens for viewing white supremacists because they provide millions of Americans with their (perhaps only) knowledge of white supremacists. I contend that the format of talk shows frames racism, as it is expressed by white supremacists, so as to make it appear contained, distant, and nonthreatening; and, the shows in which white supremacists appear distance racism by marginalizing their views in a variety of ways. First, the producers of these shows marginalize white supremacists by consistently referring to the groups as "hate groups." Shows featuring white supremacists appear with titles such as, "I'm Proud to Be a Racist," "Young Hate Mongers," "I'm Raising My Kids to be Racists," and "Hatemonger Moms." Through rhetoric such as "racist," a label that only the most committed white supremacists utilize, as well as, "hate" and "hatemonger," terms even white supremacists do not embrace, the shows signal audiences that the guests are members of a lunatic fringe bearing not the slightest connection to the vast majority of viewers. Talk-show audiences are alerted to tune in to "see what racists are like." Framing the appearance of white supremacists in this way preempts any other interrogation of racism by the audience, the host, or society at large.

Further, many of the talk shows act to contain racism by placing white supremacists on the same platform or "stage" with civil-rights leaders, arranging the show as if it were a debate. This kind of format simultaneously privileges the discourse of white supremacists by raising it to the same level as that of civil-rights leaders, while also making it seem outlandish, cartoon-like, and far removed from the experience of the audience. The "Donahue" show, for instance, featured a debate between Bill Wilkinson, then Imperial Wizard of the Ku Klux Klan, and Julian Bond, African American civil rights leader. Thus, while on the one hand, the format of the show elevates Wilkinson—and the white supremacist cause he represents—on the other, it simultaneously mocks and legitimates his cause. Even when the producers do not stage a debate, the premise is the same in other shows which feature white supremacists. In these, the host actively works to engage members of the audience and the panelists in "debate," while serving as a facilitator. The danger inherent in this is *not* that audiences will see civil rights as an "open" question, subject to debate (audiences are too sophisticated for this); instead, the danger lies in the fact that audiences (particularly white audiences) will see white supremacy as a "closed" question, settled by the civil rights movement, with only Wilkinson, and other absurd characters in outrageous costumes like him, left to defend it.

For their part, talk-show hosts and producers (along with many audience members) justify the appearance of white supremacists on the shows by arguing that by allowing them to "air" their views, reasonable people will hear them, be repulsed, and the groups will lose their appeal. As Geraldo Rivera put it, "we're exposing them to the light, and, just like cockroaches, they will run when the light is turned on." However, my reading of white supremacist publications suggests that the groups exploit their appearances on these shows to gain a measure of legitimacy and to recruit new members. The publications report receiving hundreds of letters in support of their views after each appearance. Even if we do not lend much credibility to such reports, the reports themselves offer a veneer of validity to the groups at least among their own members. The shows, for their part, gain ratings. The episode of "Geraldo" in which white supremacists and their opponents began an on-air brawl (resulting in the host's broken nose) was one of the highest-rated talk shows ever. White audiences gain a measure of superiority and distance over the vulgar displays by the panelists, again preempting any examination of their own privilege. And, given the ethic of solving social problems through talk shows—which pervades the shows—hosts, producers, and audiences can tune out feeling they have "done something about racism," without ever interrogating daily practices which reinforce white supremacy.

The appearance of white supremacists on talk shows under the guise of "debate" or the premise of "airing their views" simultaneously serves several functions. It privileges white supremacist discourse by elevating it to the level of debatable ideas while lampooning it and suggesting that the buffoonish characters on display are the last vestiges of a racist system. The shows and the white supremacist groups exist in symbiotic harmony: the shows gain ratings and the groups gain a measure of legitimacy (and a few new members)—while both espouse their dislike, distaste, and distrust for the other. For people of color in the audiences, such appearances may serve to confirm their worst fears about the persistent threat of white racism; and, more insidiously, the shows may leave them wondering how they will distinguish the avowed white supremacists from the rest of the white folks in their daily lives. And, in terms of white audiences, it lets them (us) off the proverbial racial hook because the show's message is clear: these panelists are the "racists" therefore, everyone else—all of us not on the panel, or anyone who disagrees with those on the panel—are "not racists," and hence not accountable for racial inequality. More importantly, what is left uninterrogated are the mechanisms of institutionalized white supremacy and the myriad ways individual whites benefit from and perpetuate them. The talk-show presentation of white supremacists, like the scholarly analysis of them as merely an "extremist" social movement or "deviants," precludes any broader investigation of white supremacy.

The Organizations and Their Publications

The publications I examine here represent six distinct organizations within the white supremacist movement. There are important ideological differences among the organizations. These differences are of tantamount importance to those within the organizations. Yet, despite these protestations of differences within, the organizations share a fundamental agreement in white supremacy; therefore, I use the publications interchangeably, noting distinctions where they are significant. What follows then is a brief sketch of each of the publications, along with the organizations and leaders which they represent.

The Klansman is published by the Invisible Empire, Knights of the Ku Klux Klan. The current editor of *The Klansman* is J. W. Farrands, a position that falls to whoever serves as the current Imperial Wizard at the inception of the current incarnation of the Klan in 1975 when he, along with a "small band of dedicated Klansmen," reactivated the Klan which they claim was "dormant since 1944." While under Wilkinson's control, the Invisible Empire was based in Denham Springs, Louisiana; under Farrands, the headquarters moved north to Connecticut where it remains today. The "Klan Directory" of the Invisible Empire now lists chapters, or klaverns, in Alabama, California, Florida, Georgia, Illinois, Kentucky, Mississippi, Nebraska, Nevada, Ohio, Tennessee, Virginia, and West Virginia. With their periodical in print since 1976, publishers of *The Klansman* boast that theirs is the "only publication for the white race which has never failed to publish."

The ideology espoused by *The Klansman* could be considered "mainstream" within the white supremacist movement. By this I mean that the rhetoric of *The Klansman* is less virulent than most of the publications within the study and in fact, the tone of *The Klansman* tends to be almost innocuous when compared to that of other white supremacist publications. Much of the content of *The Klansman* is organizational news (fund drives, "member of the month" columns, youth activities, and meeting reports) analogous to any other organizational publication.

The Newspaper of the National Association for the Advancement of White People (NAAWP) began in 1982 with the formation of the organization of the same name (NAWWP) by David Duke in New Orleans, Louisiana. In the 1970s, Duke was affiliated with Wilkinson's organization, the Invisible Empire, Knights of the Ku Klux Klan, but left the organization in 1978 and formed his own faction of the Ku Klux Klan. Eventually discouraged by the Klan's inability to recruit a broad spectrum of members or the prospect for ever doing so, Duke left the organization and founded the NAAWP in 1981. The NAAWP has sometimes been referred to as "the Klan without the robes and ritual" and in many ways this is true (Zatarain, 1990). Of the white supremacist groups in existence today, Duke's NAAWP is the one organization that has been able to garner relatively widespread support, clearly evidenced in the success of Duke's political campaigns (Applebome, 1991). The rhetoric in the *NAAWP* is the most restrained of those in the sample. The tone of the publication is, for white supremacist organizations, subtle, reasoned, and sophisticated. The *NAAWP* is clearly directed at a mainstream audience, hoping to attract people who would never consider donning a klan robe but are quite comfortable with many of the assumptions of white supremacy.

The Torch is published by Thom Robb of Bass, Arkansas, and represents the branch of the white supremacist movement known as Christian Identity. Robb's organization has close ties to the Invisible Empire of the Ku Klux Klan. References to the Klan are common in *The Torch*.

Robb also has ties to David Duke's NAAWP. Although direct mentions of the NAAWP are rare within the pages of *The Torch*, Robb has been significantly influenced by David Duke. He first met Duke in New Orleans in the 1970s. It was there that Duke recruited Robb into his modified version of the Klan. More recently, Robb has been following Duke's example in other ways. Robb ran for statewide political office in Arkansas in 1991, with much less success than Duke. Undaunted by his loss, Robb has begun a school for training other white supremacists who have mainstream political ambitions. According to Robb, "Louisiana has one David Duke. We plan to give America 1,000 of them."

Thom Robb was born in Detroit to a father who was a builder and a mother who worked as a department-store sales clerk. The Robb family moved to Tucson while Thom was a teenager. Thom was reportedly greatly influenced by his mother's right-wing political ideology and avidly read tracts of the John Birch Society. Robb attended a seminary in Colorado and was ordained as a Baptist minister. It is in his capacity as a minister of a brand of theology known as Christian Identity that Robb has become a leader of the white supremacist movement. "We are the glue that binds together many, many groups of like-minded kindred who for the first time are learning to pull together for their common goals under the banner of Identity," Robb said (*Chicago Tribune,* July 20, 1986, C1).

Christian Identity theology is descended from a nineteenth-century belief known as Anglo-Israelism, which holds that white Europeans and their American descendants are God's true chosen people, while Blacks and Jews are the "seed of Satan."

Identity theology derives from a book by Edward Hine, *Identification of the British Nation with Lost Israel,* published in England in 1871. According to this text, those described in the Bible as "Israelites" left the Middle East in 700 B.C., traveling north through the Caucasus Mountains until they arrived and settled in the British Isles. Thus, Caucasians, including Anglo-Saxons, Celts, and Scandinavians, are the "true Jews" while the people known today as Jews actually are a Mongolian Turkish race called Kazars descended directly from Satan. Notable biblical figures such as Moses, Abraham, and Jesus were not Jews. These, along with all white people, are descendants of Adam through his son, Abel, while all Jews are descendants of Satan through his son, Cain, who was fathered by the Serpent. The praise given by God in the Bible for God's "chosen people" refers to white people, and the wrath for infidels refers to Jews. Identity theology teaches that God created "the yellow race, brown race, and red race" on the Third Day and that they were not given souls. Only Adam and Eve and their "seed" were given souls when they were created on the Sixth Day.

In addition to Robb, Ralph Forbes is a contributing editor to *The Torch*. Forbes regularly writes features for *The Torch* and is perhaps best known as an abortion opponent who recently filed suit against the University of Arkansas Medical Sciences Hospital in an unsuccessful bid to stop pregnancy terminations.

The *Thunderbolt* (renamed *Truth at Last* in 1989) presents, as its subtitle indicates, "the white man's viewpoint." The *Thunderbolt* is published by Dr. Ed Fields, a chiropractor, and is registered as a nonprofit corporation in Georgia (Fields is also listed as the secretary of the organization). Reported to be a "quiet, soft-spoken, family man," Fields, the son of a corporate executive and a housewife, grew up in Marietta, Georgia. A former altar boy, Fields attended a Catholic high school and even won an award for religious devotion because of his practice of attending mass four times a week. After high school, Fields briefly attended law school before going to Palmer School of Chiropractic in Davenport, Iowa. He returned to Georgia to establish his chiropractic practice.

The *Thunderbolt* was founded by, and still has strong ties to, J. B. Stoner of the National States Rights' Party (NSRP), which began in 1958. Stoner, also from Marietta, was born in 1922 and started out his career as an attorney. Long associated with white supremacist causes, he was an officer of the Ku Klux Klan when he was eighteen years old and acted as legal counsel for James Earl Ray, the man who assassinated Dr. Martin Luther King, Jr. Over the years, Stoner made several unsuccessful bids for governor of Georgia, and one for state senate.

In 1980, Stoner was convicted in the 1958 bombing of Bethel Baptist Church in Birmingham, Alabama, where Rev. Shuttlesworth, a prominent civil rights leader, was pastor. Stoner was sentenced to ten years and was a fugitive for four months in 1983 before he turned himself over to the FBI to begin his prison term. Stoner was released in 1987 for "good behavior" after having served only three and a half years of his sentence. Stoner was disbarred in 1984 as a consequence of his conviction.

The content of the *Thunderbolt* is similar to that of *The Klansman*, with monthly publication of an "NSRP Member's Page" which features organizational news. However, it focuses on national and world news. The front pages of the *Thunderbolt* are filled with pictures of government and political leaders. Feature articles detail current news stories, always with an eye toward giving the "untold" story behind the news, reporting insights into the "Jewish power behind" the story with tabloid-style headlines. Although the *Thunderbolt* sees itself as part of the larger white supremacist movement, it does have ongoing disputes with other branches of the movement. For instance, the *Thunderbolt* published a report that Bill Wilkinson (formerly of *The Klansman*) was an FBI informant. As this instance indicates, divisions with the white supremacist movement are often based on personalities rather than ideologies. The *Thunderbolt* and the NSRP are believed to have ties to various Klan factions and to neo-Nazi groups both in the United States and in Europe.

Racial Loyalty was until 1993 published by Ben Klassen, a former Mennonite, and represents the branch of the white supremacist movement known as "Creativity." Klassen founded the Church of the Creator (COTC) in 1973. Born in the Ukraine to Mennonite parents, Klassen emigrated to Canada and then to the United States in the 1950s. He was reported to be a millionaire from his career as a real-estate broker in Florida. In the early 1960s, he joined the John Birch Society. When the Republican slate swept Broward County in 1965, Klassen was elected to the Florida House.

In 1968 Klassen was Florida's chairman of presidential candidate George Wallace's American Independent Party. He later concluded that Wallace was a "phony." Disenchanted with Republicans and Birchers, Klassen formed the Nationalist White Party. When his attacks on Christianity offended some members, he decided a racial "religion" was the answer. Klassen said: "I asked myself, what the hell can you believe in? And the answer was the laws of nature." He argues that the laws of nature set white people at the top of "the biological heap." He expanded on that idea in extravagant detail in the eight books, dozens of pamphlets, and monthly installments of *Racial Loyalty*.

Klassen is known as the Pontifex Maximus of the Church of the Creator (COTC). In the COTC, the worship of the white race is the central tenet. Creativity is both violently anti-Semitic and actively anti-Christian, since Judaism and all forms of Christianity are viewed as distracting whites from their "racial religion." The COTC has no liturgy and holds no service, but does hold an IRS exemption. Creativity predicts and advocates a racial holy war, in which whites and "black/mud/jew" people will fight for control of the planet. The COTC moved from Florida to the North Carolina hills of Macon County in 1982, where it remained until Klassen turned control over the group to Rick McCarty in 1993. In August 1993, Klassen committed suicide.

Creativity is the newest, and according to Klanwatch, one of the fastest growing segments of the white supremacist movement. Although based in Otto, North Carolina, the publication claims a worldwide readership and return addresses listed for letters to the editor seem to support this claim. Letters come from New Zealand, Australia, Peru, Germany, France, and South Africa.

WAR, an acronym for White Aryan Resistance, is published by Tom Metzger, a television repairman, in Fallbrook, California, and has been a popular publication among neo-Nazis and Skinheads. Metzger, as leader of the California branch of the Ku Klux Klan, was elected as the democratic nominee for the state legislature in 1980, but lost in the general elections. After he lost the congressional race, Metzger formed his own White American Political Association (WAPA). In 1984, he claimed to have a nationwide membership of between 5,000 and 10,000 in the WAPA. White American Resistance, listed as "an arm of" the WAPA, was originally the publisher of the periodical *WAR.* The name change to White *Aryan* Resistance reflects Metzger's personal disaffection with the United States government, which he claims no longer represents the interests of white people because it is a "Zionist Occupied Government," or "ZOG."

Like Duke, Metzger was dissatisfied with the Klan's ability to attract new members so he left the Klan to "go underground and try to draw from a larger base" than just Southern whites. This strategy clearly worked. WAR's current organizational roster lists affiliates in California, Delaware, Florida, Idaho, Illinois, Montana, Missouri, New York, North Carolina, Tennessee, and Texas. Metzger claims he is "much more active and more powerful than he ever was as a Klan leader." At one time, Metzger maintained close ties to Duke, but now he considers Duke a sell-out to his mainstream political ambitions. Publication of *WAR* stopped in 1991 because of a lawsuit brought by Morris Dees' Southern Poverty Law Center against Metzger for his role in the beating death of an Ethiopian man. Publication resumed briefly in 1992, then stopped again while Metzger served a six-month jail term for participating in a cross-burning.

Despite distinctions between the various segments of the white supremacist movement, these organizations share a broad ideological commitment to the notion that the white race is an essential identity, rooted in biological and "scientific" fact, and that being "white" is ontologically superior to being "Black," "Jewish," or anything other than "white." These notions of racial identity are crafted within the discourse of the publications and are forged along with notions of gender and sexuality.

3

Visions of Masculinity, Glimpses of Femininity: White Men and White Women

The discovery of personal whiteness among the world's peoples is a very modern thing—a nineteenth and twentieth century matter, indeed. The ancient world would have laughed at such a distinction. . . . Today . . . the world . . . has discovered that it is white and by that token, wonderful!

—*W. E. B. Du Bois*, Darkwater, *1920*

In 1993, *Newsweek* magazine featured a cover story entitled "White Male Paranoia—Are They the Newest Victims or Just Bad Sports?" (Gates, 1993). The article reported on the growing sentiment among white males that they are under attack, bearing the brunt of social and cultural change in the United States. Apparently, white men have discovered their "personal whiteness" (in Du Bois's terms)—and, I would add, their white masculinity—and found that it is no longer "wonderful," but, instead, ordinary.

Indeed, the challenges of the 1960s and 1970s from a variety of political movements (e.g., on the part of Blacks, Chicano/as, American Indians, women's groups, and lesbians and gay men) effectively called into question not only "whiteness," but also "white masculinity" and the normative constraints implicit in white-, male-, and heterosexual-centered analyses and foci of power. While such challenges have succeeded in making explicitly racist claims socially unacceptable, this change may signify that such sentiments have merely been subordinated, rather than eliminated, and given voice only in a cultural and ideological space designated as "extremist."

33

In sharp contrast to the subtle, often covert, forms of racism that seem to predominate today (Feagin, 1991; Jhally & Lewis, 1992; Feagin & Sikes, 1994), white supremacists are openly and explicitly racist. While these groups and their ideas are often dismissed as part of a "lunatic fringe" of political extremism, I want to suggest that they be taken seriously as a site of ideological struggle that shares much in common with more widely accepted representations of race and gender. An important place to begin is with the chief architects of white supremacist discourse—white men—by decoding the portraits they sketch of themselves.

White Men in White Supremacist Discourse

The centrality of white men in white supremacist discourse is epitomized by an illustration regularly published in *WAR* (see figure III.1). The image is of a white man, with airplanes and bridges in the background, and the accompanying text reads, "White Men *Built* This Nation, White Men *Are* This Nation!" (emphasis in the original). The image conveys several messages. It signals a link between race, "whiteness," and masculinity, specifically "white men," such that white men are the central, indeed the *only* actors visible. Even though the appeal in the illustration is one intended for all whites, both men and women, it is men who occupy the privileged position here. White women's contributions, either independently from white men or in concert with them, are effaced.

Further, the image points to a connection between white masculinity and class position; the white men to which the illustration

Figure III.1

presumably refers are those materially involved in "building" an infra-structure, those who literally "built" the bridges, airplanes, and skyscrapers featured in the background. Meanwhile the image simultaneously obliterates the labor of racial and ethnic minorities, both men and women, whose labor did, in fact, build this country. The working-class position of the man in the drawing is further signified by his attire: he is dressed in what appears to be a work shirt, vest, and hard hat, all signifiers of a working-class position. The illustration can also be read as referring to middle-class white men; those white men who researched, engineered, and developed the bridges, airplanes, and skyscrapers. Again, such a reading eliminates from view the contributions of people of color and white women to such technology. Further, it completely elides the material advantages of white men which have allowed them to produce such technology. These advantages are gained at the expense of white women, whose domestic and emotional labor as wives is appropriated, and people of color, who are effectively eliminated from competition with white men by a system of *de facto* segregation which ensures their exclusion from schools, universities, and the labor force, and whose labor is also exploited as laborers, domestics, launderers, and fast-food workers.

White masculinity here is also attached to a particular sense of nationalism, which, in this instance, signifies the conventional geographic boundaries of the United States. Here, "nation" is synonymous with "whiteness" and working- or middle-class masculinity. This one image, then, demonstrates many of the linkages between whiteness, masculinity, class, and nationalism in white supremacist discourse. However, the boundaries of race, gender, class, and nation do not fit together quite so seamlessly elsewhere in this discourse. The construction of white men as warriors reveals the multi-faceted dimensions of these dynamics.

The white man in this illustration stands tall, his posture indicating that his body is as erect and impenetrable as the buildings in the background. Thus, this one white man comes to represent all white (heterosexual) men, who are—within the context of white supremacist discourse—the embodiment of the phallic will and conscious control, and hence, deserving of respect or even worship (Bordo, 1993:701–2).

White Warriors, White "Victims"

White men are portrayed as racial warriors within white supremacist discourse, both offensively, against particular enemies, and defensively, as protectors of the white race from outside attacks. Analogous to the "soldier/males" depicted in the imagery of the *friekorps* of interwar Germany,

Figure III.2

the image of white men as "racial warriors" is a prevalent one in contemporary white supremacist publications (Theweleit, 1987). Though the racial warrior is woven throughout the publications, both *Racial Loyalty* and *WAR* draw on this metaphor much more heavily than do any others (see figure III.2). The leitmotif of *Racial Loyalty* is one of impending racial war and the need for white men to unite as warriors in this conflict. The rallying cry of "Creators" (members of the Church of the Creator, the racial religion advocated by *Racial Loyalty*) is "RAHOWA!" which stands for "RAcial HOly WAr." And, clearly, the choice of the acronym *WAR* is indicative of this imagery.

Here again, we see the conflation of "whiteness" and masculinity demonstrating the inextricable connection between race and gender. However, the warrior valorizes a form of white masculinity slightly differ-

36

ent from that in the previous image. The caption above the drawing, "Let's Kick Some Ass!" indicates the violence inherent in extremist white supremacist discourse and organizations. It is also representative of a particular form of masculinity in which violence is equated with masculinity (Connell, 1987). The warrior, with his shirtless, hairless chest, chiseled jawline, and blonde hair, evokes the Aryan ideal of "whiteness" and represents the conflation of violence and masculinity.

Gender, race, and nation are again conflated but configured differently here than above. Rather than a simple equation of race with the United States, "nation" is fragmented and subsumed under "race." Flags representing both the United States and Great Britain figure prominently in the drawing and are set against the backdrop of a city skyline. The warrior pictured gives a Nazi salute in front of a swastika, signifying links to Germany's Nazi past and to contemporary movements of neo-Nazis and Skinheads, as indicated in the caption below.

By foregrounding the white racial warrior over the images of three different nations, "whiteness," specifically white masculinity, is asserted across national boundaries as more salient than identification with each nation. By linking the images in this way, the geographic boundaries of nations are simultaneously invoked and called into question, while white masculinity is affirmed as more worthy of loyalty than any particular nation.

White men are not uniformly depicted in white supremacist discourse as the embodiment of strength which the warrior imagery indicates. The very notion of "warrior" is one that exists within a dualistic construction and depends on its juxtaposition to the view of white men as "victims." On almost every front in which white men are presented as "warriors" they are simultaneously presented as "victims." White men depict themselves as victims of racial discrimination, of class oppression, and as the special victims of race, gender, and class oppression at the hands of the racial state. The white warrior who protects his family may find himself a victim of the state, and his family may be the victim of racial Others. And, in an ironic twist on the traditional depictions of white women as sexual victims of Black men, white men also depict themselves as victims, or potential victims, of both physical and sexual assault by Black men.

The chief enemies in white supremacist discourse are racialized Others. The primary figures are African Americans, constructed as possessors of "Blackness," an essence depicted as the antithesis of "whiteness;" and Jews, possessors of a "Jewish" essence, also set out in opposition to "whiteness." White supremacist discourse nourishes a worldview in which a global racial war is imminent, and indeed, inevitable. In this war, the "white race" will be led into battle by white men to fight against all the "dark hordes" which threaten to destroy a planet white supremacists envision as exclusively theirs. The image of the triumphant white warrior is constructed in opposition to the view of white men as victims of racial Others, especially Black men.

White men portray themselves as victims of potential or actual physical attack. This imagery is woven throughout the text of the publications and is apparently such a powerful image that *The Torch* uses an illustration of a white man being physically assaulted by several Black men as a recruiting device (see figure III.3). The image appears on the last page of each issue of *The Torch*, next to the membership application. Above it is the caption, "It's your Move." The juxtaposition of image and text invokes the threat of physical violence and gets to a central feature of white supremacy, white men's fear of being physically attacked by a Black man (or, as here, a group of Black men). This fear stands in stark contrast to the image of the white man as "racial warrior," who appears virtually invincible as he fights the "dark hordes" and defends the white face. White men's fear of victimization is not only physical, it is also sexual.

Figure III.3

Stories of sexual attacks on white men by Black men are rife throughout the publications. One story describes the plight of a young white man:

> Young Bryan and Kevin Johnson was brutally raped by negroes Gary and Raymond Davis. Then the two African butchers crudely cut off Bryan's penis and testicles and stuffed them down the struggling youth's throat. (*Thunderbolt*, no. 261, 1981, p. 1)

Here, with horrid detail, the *Thunderbolt* provides a vivid description of the potential physical and sexual attacks to which white men imagine themselves falling victim, and reinforces the image of white men as victims and Black men as predators. The emphasis on the white man as "young" and "struggling" heightens the portrayal of him as a victim; characterizing the attack as "brutal" and the men involved as "negroes" and "African butchers" strengthens the image of Black men as savages.

Placing this incident about one white man in the context of a white supremacist publication serves to eclipse the reality that literally thousands of Black men were hunted, tortured, castrated, and murdered at the hands of whites (especially, though not exclusively, white *men*) in the United States during the reign of terror known as lynching. At the same time, it serves to obscure the racial, sexual, and class politics that were central to the ideological justification of lynching, in which white women were constructed as sexually chaste and powerless victims at the hands of mythically bestial and rapacious Black men.

While not eliminating the image of white women as sexual victims of Black men (this is still a central feature of white supremacist discourse), contemporary constructions have amended white men onto this centuries-old racial iconography. Now, white men also see themselves as potential victims of sexual assault by brutish Black men. The extension of white supremacist ideology to include white men as potential victims illustrates the pervasive fear of Black sexuality which is fundamental to white supremacy (Collins, 1990:78; West, 1993:86).

[handwritten margin note: White fear of black sexuality]

The fear of Black sexuality intensifies when it is combined with homophobia. This is evident in articles which claim to report on the experiences of white men who are incarcerated. In keeping with the warrior imagery, all white men in United States prisons, because they are imprisoned by the racial state and forced to reside with inmates who are not white, are seen as "political prisoners." One article states that Black men "force homosexualism on white slave prisoners" (*Thunderbolt*, no. 255, 1980, p. 6). As in other settings, in the context of prison life it is Black men who are constructed as rapists. White men's victim status is affirmed by their representation not only as "prisoners" but also as "slave prisoners." Such a reference, like the one above to the castration and murder of a young white man, acts to reverse the history of American racial politics by positioning white men as "slaves" and Black men as sexual predators while simultaneously reinforcing the myth of the Black male rapist. It seems clear that the threat of homosexuality implied is intended to make the sexual threat of Black men to white men *even more serious* than the supposed threat to white women. Given this seriousness, it is not surprising then that protecting white heterosexuality is considered key to the protection of white families.

The highest duty and honor of a white man, according to white supremacist discourse, is to preserve the white family and with it a hierarchy of race, gender, and sexuality. Much of the text highlights the theme of white men as protectors of "kin and family even unto death" (*WAR*, vol. 4, no. 3, 1985, p. 10). The *NAAWP*, for instance, features the article, "An American Tragedy," which tells the story of a white man who is jailed because he killed a Black man for allegedly raping and murdering his wife (*NAAWP*, no. 22, 1982, p. 13). Here, the specter of the Black man as savage rapist and murderer is invoked to buttress the notion that white men are the legitimate protectors, even avengers, of white women who are ensconced in white, heterosexual, nuclear families.

A drawing that regularly appears in the *Thunderbolt* can be read in this context (see figure III.4). In this illustration, symbols of white supremacy frame a white family. This image conveys a profusion of messages and gives some hints as to the linkages between white supremacy, gender, and sexuality. The man in the drawing holds a gun and assumes a protective stance in front of the woman and two children. He is placed in the dominant, foregrounded position, thus reinforcing male-dominance. The appearance of the gun in this context makes sense given the construction of the warrior and can be read as a symbol of male-centered authority associated with the father, or patriarch, within the family. The juxtaposition of the gun and the "family" can also be read as buttressing the patriarchal "ownership" of women and children. The gun can be further understood as the phallus which guards the terrain of heterosexuality inscribed within the white family.

The woman in the drawing appears in a subordinate position, slightly behind the man and holding onto his arm, connoting her location within the familial hierarchy. She is clad in a dress and apron, signifying a type of

Figure III.4

domesticity associated with "true womanhood." The apron further signals the appropriation of her labor within the family. The woman's appearance in a dress, attire associated with propriety (when worn by women), can be regarded as a symbol of her sexual purity and chastity. For white women, sexual purity and chastity are defined in white supremacist discourse as (hetero)sexual activity exclusively with white, heterosexual men, typically within the confines of the family. Further evidence of her racially appropriate sexuality is furnished by the appearance of the children in the drawing. The children provide a reading of the woman as "mother," a position privileged within white supremacist discourse when it is occupied by white women. The beatific qualities attributed to white motherhood in these texts are constructed in sharp contrast to the images of Black women who appear as "welfare queens" and unqualified mothers.

Behind both mother and father stand the two children. The inclusion of children in the drawing can be read as providing further testimony to the procreative mission of the white family, reproducing the white race. The placement of *two* children, a boy and a girl, is significant. The stance of the children reinforces notions of male-dominance, for even though the girl appears to be older and taller, she is set in the background while the boy is placed in the dominant position in the foreground. The location of a male and a female child in the image reinscribes notions of male/female dualism, and with it, heterosexuality.

The family is bracketed by two symbols; to the left a cross appears within a circle surrounded by text which reads: "God Bless America." The symbolism here conflates nation and "God" in such a way that religion, specifically Christianity, and the United States are equivalent. This is one instance in which ideas of "God" and nation are combined as justifications for the ideologies of race, gender, and sexuality established in the white family. However, this connection by no means holds for all white supremacist ideologies. In fact, ideas concerning "God" or religion and nation represent one of the major cleavages for white supremacist discourse and organizations.[1] Nevertheless, in this instance, the two come together to valorize a particular conceptualization of the family, and with it, a particular hierarchy of race, gender, and sexuality.

On the opposite side of the drawing is a symbol of a thunderbolt, encircled by the slogan "White Power." As throughout white supremacist discourse, "whiteness" is asserted as a pure essence, held by a select few, and claimed here as a powerful virtue. Appearing as it does alongside the drawing of the family, the slogan asserts a value to white families over other, "non-white" families. The choice of the thunderbolt symbol (which is also the name of the publication in which this illustration appears, and is repeated in the drawing of the sun) invokes notions of "the natural or-

41

der" of the universe, premised on dualisms such as male/female, white/black, "God"/man. In such a universe, white, heterosexual families are central.

Enclosed by symbols of race, nation, and "God," this illustration can be read as embodying the ideal of the white, heterosexual, procreative, nuclear family. The rhetoric surrounding the defense of the family represents an entire nexus of ideologies about gender and sexuality. The protection of "the family" is a code for the protection of white male authority, the appropriation of white women's labor in the home, the production and ownership of white children, and the insured continuation of heterosexuality.

The image of the white, heterosexual, procreative, nuclear family depicted in extremist white supremacist discourse reverberates forcefully throughout the culture at large. Indeed, remove the symbols which frame the drawings in the illustration depicted here (and perhaps the gun, though not necessarily), and you are left with an image of "the family" which has become a central feature in mainstream political discourse about "family values" in the 1980s and 1990s.

In an astonishing (and unprecedented) move, a sitting Vice President of the United States used the importance of his office and the platform of a political speech to launch an attack against a character on a prime-time situation comedy. I am, of course, referring to the controversy provoked by then Vice President Dan Quayle's charge that the character "Murphy Brown," portrayed on television by Candace Bergen, was emblematic of the decline in "family values." Quayle's concern was that Murphy Brown, the unmarried lead *character* (not Ms. Bergen herself, dutifully married in reality), was having a child. In Quayle's view, this example would lead to all manner of deleterious ends among them: it would make single motherhood "acceptable" and would lead other unmarried women to do the same; and this would lead inexorably to a devaluation of "the family." Clearly, Quayle's statements were intended to reinforce a particular form of family—the same narrow conceptualization of the family heralded by white supremacist discourse—and to sanction attempts at creating other forms. More recently, Speaker of the House Newt Gingrich's proposals to remove children from their homes if they are headed by single mothers is another example of the attempt to use the power of the state to enforce the patriarchal family. While Dan Quayle's remarks sparked a good deal of spirited public discourse about Murphy Brown's example as a positive one (including bumper stickers which read "Murphy Brown for President," and the incorporation of the dispute into a story line) and Speaker Gingrich eventually backed down from his proposal for establishing orphanages for the children of single mothers, the fact that two highly ranked, popularly elected, incumbent, government officials could make such assertions is evidence of how effectively the themes of white supremacist discourse resonate within mainstream political discourse.

White Supremacy, Class, and the Racial State

Class is an important issue in white supremacist ideologies and one which is embedded in issues of race and gender. Much of the focus in these publications is on working-class issues, such as a special issue of *WAR* published in 1985 which was addressed to the "White Worker." Such a focus reflects the working-class position of many of those in the white supremacist movement.[2] However, given the broadening appeal of the white supremacist movement, it is not exclusively working-class.[3] What emerges in the discourse is a melding of working- and middle-class concerns forged in opposition to an elite class, associated with corporations and the government, and in opposition to racialized Others who may also be members of the working-middle classes. Class is not, however, separable from race and gender.

Concerns about class merge with issues of race and gender in the following drawing which appears frequently in several of the publications (see figure III.5). In this image, three menacing figures appear, each one a caricature of a racialized group. On the left, is a Jewish man, denoted by the exaggeratedly pointed nose; on the right is a Hispanic man,[4] designated by the moustache and

Figure III.5

43

large *sombrero*; and in the center, an African American man appears, marked by a large afro hairstyle, a broad nose, and large lips. The drawing is framed at the top by the caption, "White Man Beware!" and at the bottom by the ominous warning, supposedly spoken by the three central figures, "We Want Your Jobs, Your Homes, Your Country, Wake Up!"

In this instance, white male workers are constructed as under attack from Jewish, African American, and Hispanic men. It is significant to note that the conflict as it is framed here is not between all "whites" and all Jewish, African American, or Hispanic people (though this is certainly the implication); rather, it is specifically *men*—Jewish men, African American men, and Hispanic men—who are constructed as "threats" to white men. In this way, masculinity becomes racialized and race becomes masculinized.

Gender is further implicated in that one of the major arenas of threat is to the homes of white men. The notion of "home" again conjures up a vision of the nuclear family mentioned previously; and, it is within this "home" that white women are located. The notion that white men's "homes" are threatened by Jewish, African American, and Hispanic men elicits the myth of the need for the chivalrous protection of white heterosexual women by white heterosexual men.

Class issues are woven together with those of race and gender in this image. It is the threat to white men's jobs, and thus to their concerns about their class position, which may be read as central here, because it is "jobs" which are placed first in the catalogs of perils to white men. Further, jobs are symbolic of masculinity, especially (though by no means exclusively) working-class masculinity, associated more closely with "jobs" than "careers." These jobs are also inscribed with race, as they point to a specific construction of white masculinity, in which white men view themselves as exclusively entitled to jobs. And, unlike calls to transcend national boundaries through race, this image calls up the conventional borders of the United States. The community within the image calls up the conventional borders of the United States. The community within these barriers is imagined to be one exclusively reserved for white citizens. Thus, the illustration fuses the construction of racialized Others and gender with class and nation in a context which evokes the white man as warrior, "defending" white jobs, a white country, and white homes.

Still, class issues are most often set out as the white workers' (whether blue-collar or white-collar) struggle against a powerful elite class. It is corporations, a symbol of elite class privilege allied with government, which are often cast as enemies of the white race, as in the article, "White Corporate Renegades Sell Out Future Generations!" (*Torch*, vol. 10, no. 4, 1979, pp. 1–3).

Conceptualizations of class and state converge in white supremacist discourse in the characterization of the United States government as the "Zionist Occupation Government" (ZOG). White supremacists view the government as a racial state which consistently privileges minority group members over whites (Omi, 1990). While this is certainly an important aspect of the "racialized" nature of the state, in these writings it is not the only way in which the state is seen as a racial entity. As indicated by the ubiquitous reference to the state as "ZOG" ("Zionist" is equated with "Jewish") within these publications, the state is depicted as inherently "Jewish," a racial identity within the discourse. The government, as well as the corporate elite, is supposedly "occupied" and controlled by Jews. This racial view of the state is also inherently gendered in that it is specifically Jewish men who are in the positions of power. This conflated vision of class and racial state is gendered in other ways as well.

White supremacists contend that it is primarily the government that interferes with the white man's duty to protect his family. In an article from *WAR* called "It's the Law," which derides white men as dupes for obeying laws that are the creation of and serve the interests of "ZOG," Metzger writes:

> When it becomes the law of the land that every White man with a daughter between 12 and 17 years of age, must bring her to an inter-racial bi-sexual sensitivity class he will obey, for it is the law. There his daughter will alternately be raped and sodomized by Negroes and bull dyke Jewesses . . . (*WAR*, vol. 4, no. 3, 1985, p. 10)

Metzger's comment reflects a view in which the state is not only a racial entity, but also a specifically gendered one. The state as presented here is implicated in the potential failure of white men to protect their families and in the rape of their young white daughters.

Affirmative action is a frequent target of white supremacist rhetoric and one which brings together views of the racial state, class, race, and gender. Affirmative-action programs are always seen as top-down, government imposed, quota systems. Under such systems, it is mandated that the most qualified white man cannot be hired for a job if even one minority, however unqualified (and minorities are, by definition, unqualified) applies for the same job. This view of affirmative action contrasts sharply with what affirmative action has, in actuality, meant; that is, limited, patchwork programs adopted by many businesses and organizations, certainly some more enthusiastically than others, to redress an entrenched and pervasive system of racial discrimination. According to white supremacist

[handwritten margin note: Affirmative action]

discourse it is white men who are targeted by these programs on the basis of race, gender, and class.

White men are depicted as the special victims of the state and of government affirmative action policies. If the intent of white supremacists is to gain support among all whites, we might expect to see discussion of perceived discrimination against whites as a generic, ungendered category. And we do in fact see this in articles such as "Massive Racial Discrimination Against Whites" (*NAAWP*, no. 31, 1984, pp. 4–60).

However, affirmative-action programs do not affect all whites equally; indeed, such programs benefit white women. Interestingly, this fact is never acknowledged by *NAAWP*, a publication which regularly features articles on affirmative action. Instead, what *NAAWP* and other publications do in stories about affirmative action is highlight the particular plight of white men. For example, in "White Boys Need Not Apply," the *NAAWP* argues that white men are regularly discriminated against in hiring because of affirmative action (*NAAWP*, no. 26, 1983, p. 7; see also *NAAWP*, no. 31, 1984, pp. 4–6; *NAAWP*, no. 21, 1982, p. 5). There is scant attention given in these publications to the benefits white women receive from these programs.

Only *WAR* addresses the fact that white women benefit from affirmative-action programs, and this acknowledgment is an isolated one. The reference occurs in a story about two white, self-styled mountain men who abducted a white woman to make her the "wife" of the man. This sympathetic description of the men's plight was offered:

> The problem they faced is common to hundreds of thousands of White men at this time. As the White men drop, or are forced, out of the system, many return to the mountains or forests which fit their racial soul. The White women however, who are the most beautiful and most desired of all the females on the earth, are staying behind in the cities. There are the Jew affirmative action programs to make them economically superior to the remaining racially true White men . . . (*WAR*, vol. 4, no. 3, 1985, p. 10).

My focus here is on the last sentence of this quote which refers to affirmative-action programs. The result of these programs is to make white women "economically superior" to white men. This passing reference is the only one to address the benefits white women receive from affirmative-action programs.

Thus, within the logic of the discourse it is *white men* who suffer most at the hands of the racial state because of their race, gender, and class. For instance, *WAR* refers to the "hypocrisy of reverse discrimination" which is taking from "the White man, his job, and thus everything he owns . . ." (*WAR*, vol. 4, no. 3, 1985, p. 9). Again in *WAR* is the story of "Alan Forest," an allegory of the plight of white men. In it, "Forest" roams the country-side looking for work but cannot find it because "everywhere I went they advertised they were Equal Opportunity Employers and could not hire White males" (*WAR*, vol. 4, no. 5, 1985, p. 4). Eventually, "Forest" winds up destitute, searching dumpsters for food, and ultimately lands in jail.

Rhetoric about affirmative action similar to that in white supremacist discourse is not difficult to find in the culture at large. A cursory review of the titles of articles addressing the issue of affirmative action in the mainstream press reflect the growing disaffection: "What Price Preference?" (*Time*, Sept. 1991); "A Remedy for Old Racism Has New Kind of Shackles: Children of affirmative Action Are Ambivalent," (*New York Times*, Sept. 15, 1991, A1); and "Affirmative Action No Longer Useful," *Miami Herald*, Feb. 1, 1995). The general unpopularity of affirmative-action programs is strongest among young, white males who are most likely to see themselves as "paying an unfair penalty" because of affirmative action (Gates, *Newsweek*, 1993:52).

The resentment of affirmative-action programs among white males has had a number of consequences. A white male academic in California is leading a fight to end all hiring and admissions practices which seek to redress discrimination based on race or gender, calling such programs themselves discriminatory. And according to a recent *Wall Street Journal*/NBC poll, there is broad support for such an initiative, especially among white males. Sixty-eight percent of white males surveyed (as opposed to 61 percent of all adults) said they were in favor, in response to the question, "Do you favor or oppose eliminating affirmative action based on race or gender in deciding admissions to state universities, hiring for government jobs, and awarding federal contracts?" (Waratzman, *Wall Street Journal*, Jan. 24, 1995, A24). The article goes on to refer to "angry white males" as "the most important group" politically.

This white male anger is felt on college campuses as well. In an article for *The Chronicle of Higher Education* entitled, "Coping with the Alienation of White Male Students," Bill Dziech writes that educators have been "autocratic" in efforts to "encourage sensitivity" about race and gender (*CHE*, Jan. 13, 1995, B1–2). He cites the example of one young, white male college student, whose response he sees as characteristic of the more generalized alienation of white male students:

> You know what affirmative action means to me? It means that even with a 3.9, I have less chance of getting into med school than someone with a 3.4 who's lucky enough to be a "victim"—whatever that means.

And another:

> I guess you could say I'm mad. All they ever do around here is lecture me about how I have to care about people who would blow my brains out if they could get away with it. Nobody gives a damn about me.

Dziech does nothing in the text to challenge the implicit racist assumptions by the first student, of Black inferiority and the trivialization of institutionalization white supremacy with "victimhood," and by the second student, of Black violence and crime. In fact, the tone and focus of the article is in support of the students' assessment of the current state of affairs in higher education. Dziech goes on to suggest that the needs of white male college students have been overlooked in the rush to embrace diversity, and that we need to recognize these students' "alienation" just as we address the concerns of other groups of students. What such an approach—which equates white male students with "any other groups"—ignores is the white supremacist context which systematically benefits white male students (and white male academics).

The fact that discourse about affirmative-action programs in extremist publications converges with that in the mainstream and academic press illustrates my point that movement discourse is not far removed from other expressions of white supremacist ideology. More significantly, however, the convergence exemplifies the way white supremacist discourse, whether extremist or mainstream, serves to maintain systems of privilege. By casting *themselves* as victims of discrimination, white men, whether as avowed white supremacists or as academics, distract attention away from the white supremacist context in which they operate. This bolsters their position within that context by fostering an ideology of "individual achievement" which elides the material impact of race and gender. Further, the fact that a piecemeal program like affirmative action could be interpreted as "discrimination" against white males given the larger context of institutionalized white supremacy (set out in chapter 2), and that such an interpretation could achieve broad acceptance among "reasonable" people, is testimony to the hegemonic power of white supremacy. It is remarkable, if no less disheartening, that such a meager attempt at addressing entrenched white privilege (widely supported by whites when first introduced just twenty years ago) could be so thoroughly discredited in such a brief period of time. Whites like to point to neoconservative Blacks who are also critical of affirmative action as "proof" that they are not being "racist" when they argue for dismantling such programs. There are legitimate concerns about the problematics inherent in affirmative-action

programs such as: only a few actually benefit; the programs do not ame-
liorate, but rather reinforce, class inequality; those who do benefit, and by
extension all others in that category, are suspected of being "unqualified."
However, framing such concerns in terms of ending "discrimination"
against white males—rather than, for example, more effective means for
dismantling white male privilege—serves to sustain institutionalized white
supremacy.

Sexual Dominance and White Masculinity

White men, as the central actors in and framers of white supremacist discourse, cast themselves as engaged in conflict with Others for dominance, frequently of a
distinctly sexual na-
ture. This conflict is
taken to an extreme
in the illustration fea-
tured here (see figure
III.6). In the drawing,
a white man holds
down a Black man
with one foot, while
at the same time
sodomizing him with
a flagpole. At the
other end of the flag-
pole is a Confederate
flag.[5] Next to this im-
age is a long scroll
(not included here)
which mentions the
flag controversy and
suggests that as whites
in the past have
fought and died for this symbol, they might be so inspired again. After
asserting that Blacks cannot possibly "grasp the noble concept of pre-
serving family heritage," the text goes on to conclude:

Figure III.6

> Consequently, it's safe to say that they feel little allegiance to their
> own past family and have absolutely *no* regard, respect or under-
> standing for ours . . . But I can tell you one thing these ignorant

49

coon bastards *will* feel if they persist with their campaign to ban the
FLAG OF DIXIE! [all emphasis in the original]. (*WAR*, vol. 8, no. 3,
1989, p. 3)

The debate over the Confederate flag is framed here as a conflict between
white and Black masculinity. Even if Black men are legally successful in
banning the flag, a symbol of white "family heritage" and masculinity, the
unambiguous threat in this illustration is that white men will ultimately
triumph in a most masculinized manner, through an act of penetration.
Not coincidentally, the white man in this illustration is inflicting this vio-
lation in defense of "family heritage," an emblem of white heterosexuality. This white man can sodomize a Black man without challenging his
heterosexual credentials. Indeed, through this act of penetrating another
man he is defending (white) heterosexuality as an institution, much as
supposedly straight gay-bashing young men report sodomizing gay men
because "homosexuality is wrong" (Comstock, 1991). Of course, what
makes this valorized portrayal of a white man engaged in male-to-male
sexual contact all the more astonishing, and ironic, are the vehement attacks against homosexuality elsewhere in this discourse (as discussed further in chapter 5).

The subordination of the Black man and by extension, Black masculinity, in this drawing is located in the body. Here, the subordinated
Other, a Black man, is penetrated by a white man, the agent of penetration. As in pornography, the bodies of Others are racialized and sexualized for the purpose of penetration. Perhaps not surprisingly, white men
see themselves as in conflict with gay men of all races. White men who engage in "homosexualism" voluntarily and openly by proclaiming a gay
identity appear to be the only white men who are excluded from white
male privilege in the discourse. While race and ethnicity are not highlighted in discussions of homosexuality, neither are they completely effaced.[6] As the HIV/AIDS pandemic devastated the gay male community
in 1980s and 1990s, the image of gay men within the publications became
one conflated with sickness and disease. The drawing featured here illu-
minates this link between the threat of illness and the sense of conflict between white, heterosexual men and gay men of all races (see figure III.7).
Here, an emaciated gay man walks with a cane, while other (presumably
heterosexual) figures flee in the background. Even though this man is
gaunt and his clothes appear to be loose-fitting in general, the detail of his
pants shows a clear indentation, representative of penetration. The caption above the drawing reads, "The Last Pitiful Squeak from Any AIDS
Ravaged Fag." In a break with the conventions of distance between illustrator and illustrated, the gay man in the drawing, between gasps, makes

an accusation of homophobia toward the illustrator and, by extension, to the reader. The illustrator, in conjunction with and giving voice to the reader, responds to this accusation in a long and vitriolic diatribe, concluding with:

> So SHUT UP and take your F * N' medicine, you plague ridden pansies . . . Be a F * N' man just once in your loathsome life, will ya?!! [all emphasis in original]. (*WAR*, vol. 8, no. 3, 1989, p. 3)

In this statement about being a "man," the illustrator unequivocally demarcates masculinity, in this instance white supremacist masculinity, as that which is *not* homosexual, with that which penetrates, rather than within that which is penetrated.

Central to this definition of masculinity and its concomitant view of homosexuality is not the contour of relationships between men, but rather the body and the penetration of the body. In what can only be called a stunning juxtaposition, this drawing (fig. III.7) and the previous illustration (fig. III.6) appear on the same page of *WAR*. In the former, a white (supposedly heterosexual) man is triumphant in his masculinity through the act of penetrating a Black man; in the latter, a gay, white man is stripped of his masculinity *because* he is penetrated. The site of the body and its penetration is foremost among markers of dominance. Sexual dominance is central to pornography (Bordo, 1993; Dworkin, 1981; Kimmel, 1988; MacKinnon, 1993) and is a key element to the hegemonic form of white supremacist masculinity.

Figure III.7

White Supremacy and White Masculinity

What, then, are we to make of these images of white men? Are these the rantings of a lunatic fringe? Or, do these themes resonate within a larger cultural context? I contend that it is not coincidental that a white backlash has coincided with a male backlash. The contemporary white supremacist movement represents the convergence of reactionary responses not only to the challenges of racial minorities in the 1960s, but also to the challenges by movements of women, gays, and lesbians in the 1970s. While this discourse is most certainly a response to the challenges by minority movements to the value and the very existence of "whiteness," what has been neglected is the fact that it is white *men* who are central to the movement and to the discourse.

The construction of white men as warriors within extremist white supremacist discourse coincides with a resurgence of warrior imagery in United States society beyond the boundaries of white supremacist publications. The positioning of white men as warriors is in keeping with Theweleit's (1987) discussion of the "soldier males" of the *friekorps* who were filled with the dread of women, floods, and bodies, while enthusiastically embracing the dualism of Western culture and aligning themselves with one side and rejecting any blurring of that line. This construction of white men as warriors is not the exclusive purview of white supremacist discourse, however, Indeed, a process of "remasculinization," reclaiming the value of masculinity, has been a predominant current in United States culture since the end of the Vietnam War (Jeffords, 1989). Representations of Vietnam in popular film, such as *First Blood, Rambo; First Blood, Part II; Missing in Action; Missing in Action 2—The Beginning;* and *Uncommon Valor* have been part of this process of remasculinization. In these films, Vietnam portrayals are particularly gendered because the soldier/veteran reclaims his masculinity only in opposition to characters or institutions defined as feminine. Within white supremacist discourse, the process of remasculinization combines with the process of rearticulating whiteness to produce the white male racial warrior.

In the 1980s and 1990s, warrior imagery was a guiding metaphor in the growing men's movement. This movement appealed mainly to white middle- and upper-middle-class men who, on weekend retreats in the woods, would beat drums and share inner feelings. Robert Bly, one of the leaders of the movement, wrote *Iron John*, a national best seller. In this text, Bly urged men to get in touch with their "inner warrior."

Even more prevalent than "warriors," white men are increasingly cast as "victims." Like the dualistic construction of warriors/"victims" in white supremacist discourse, there is an increasing sense of white men as "victims" in popular culture that coincides with a growing sense of resentment among white men outside the white supremacist movement.

A study conducted on what are now referred to as "Reagan Democrats," that is, Democrats who voted for the Republican Ronald Reagan, illustrates the emerging sense of white male victimhood. Focus groups of blue-collar workers were asked, "Who do you think gets the raw deal?" These workers, all white men, answered: "We do . . . the middle-class white guy." "The average working man, male." Perhaps the most telling response of all was the following:

> 'Cause women get advantages, blacks get advantages, the Hispanics get advantages, Orientals get advantages. Everybody but the white male race gets advantages now. (Greenberg, 1985)

These workers echo what many white men in the 1980s and 1990s have reported, that they feel singled out and particularly disadvantaged. It is important to note that this disadvantage is one which is based on race, on "whiteness" as an oppressed racial category, and also on gender, specifically "maleness," as an oppressed gender category. For these men, the most disadvantaged social position is to be a member of the "white male race."

Frederick R. Lynch provides further documentation of this growing sense of white male victim-status in *Invisible Victims: White Males and the Crisis of Affirmative Action* (1991). As the title indicates, Lynch sets out to make a case for white males as victims, examining, in his words, the "social psychological impact of affirmation action policies on white males" (1991:4). Not surprisingly, Lynch finds support for this from the 32 white men he interviewed in the mid-1980s for the book.

The phenomena of white male resentment is not one restricted to blue-collar workers, to Reagan Democrats, or to the 1980s. The 1993 *Newsweek* magazine cover story on "White Male Paranoia," mentioned at the beginning of this chapter, reported that white men are feeling increasingly embattled. In a survey conducted especially for this issue by the Gallup organization, *Newsweek* documents many of the sentiments of white males. When asked "Are white men losing influence in American society today?" 48 percent of white males, versus 35 percent of the entire sample, responded "yes." When asked, "Are white men losing an advantage in terms of jobs and income?" 56 percent of white males, versus 38 percent of the total sample, said "yes." And when asked, "Are white males losing influence over American culture—style, entertainment, and the arts?" 52 percent of white males, versus 37 percent of the entire sample, responded "yes." Clearly, white men see themselves as not merely embattled, but also as victims of a changing society.

Ready and willing to fuel this discontent are two radio personalities with enormously popular talk shows. In November 1993, *Time* magazine ran a cover story on Howard Stern and Rush Limbaugh, reported to be the "Voice of America." Between them, Stern and Limbaugh claim millions of daily listeners (and each boasts several million readers of their best-selling books) who thrive on their daily dose of bigotry and misogyny. Stern and Limbaugh remain most popular among white men.

Again, the process of remasculinization of the culture since the Vietnam War is worth examining here. Because of their association with the only war the United States has ever lost, Vietnam veterans became emblems of loss, moral failure, or national decline. Thus, representations of Vietnam in popular culture could effectively portray these soldier/veterans, like the white male warrior/victims imagined within white supremacist discourse, as "victims" of the war, society, and most especially, the government. Thus, an important shift takes place: white men ". . . were not oppressors but instead, along with women and men of color, themselves victims of a third oppressor, in this case the government" (Jeffords 1989:185). It makes sense, then, that the chief opponent in the popular film representations of the Vietnam War is not only the Vietnamese people, but also the United States government. So it is in white supremacist discourse; the primary opponents of white men are not only racial Others, but also the government.

The rhetoric of Limbaugh and Stern, the "white male paranoia" documented by *Newsweek,* and the sentiments of the Reagan Democrats or those in Lynch's study, all express a sense of white male victimhood, a sentiment shared with the white men in white supremacist discourse. What then are we to make of this convergence between white men within this discourse and more mainstream representations of white men?

The use of warrior imagery within white supremacist discourse, the men's movement, and popular films is indicative of the increasing consolidation of white, middle-class, heterosexual men's interests. The racial warrior in white supremacist discourse envisions himself embattled against "feminizing forces" just as those in the men's movement do. The racial warrior of the white supremacist movement perceives himself to be a noble freedom fighter waging a just war against the "non-white" hordes, much like the Vietnam solider/veteran depicted in recent films, as well as the embattled Everyman typified by Michael Douglas's character in the film, *Falling Down.* Indeed, the overlap between white supremacist discourse and that of more mainstream representations of white men is neither a coincidence nor simply the appropriation of these images by white supremacists.

Rather, this confluence reflects the increasing consolidation of white men's interests against real changes in the demographic composition of United States society, estimates of which indicate that by the year 2000, white men will be a numerical "minority"; in the economic structure, in which well-paid, blue-collar manufacturing and mid-level managerial jobs are increasingly replaced by low-paying, pink-collar, service-sector jobs; and, in changing cultural expectations, in which white men, especially white heterosexual men, report feeling increasingly adrift in what they perceive to be the sea of "political correctness." In this way, the racial warriors of the white supremacist movement are little different from the "warriors" in the men's movement, the "warriors" featured in *Rambo*, or the Every-white-man featured in *Falling Down*.

The confluence of images is an indication of the very real threat felt by white men to a changing economy, to demographic changes, and, potentially, though by no means certainly, a subsequent change in the system for distributing social rewards in which white men have traditionally received the lion's share of the benefits. It is also evidence of the growing sense in which white men within the white supremacist movement and the men's movement, as well as Democratic defectors, blue-collar men within the Democratic party who supported the Reagan/Bush administrations, and Limbaugh and Stern devotees, are beginning to see themselves as an authentic political constituency. And they are mobilizing on the basis of their shared, essential identity as members of the "white male race." As uncomfortable as such an association may be, the increasing sense of identity and the consolidation of interests among white, heterosexual men is a fact which bridges the gap between some Limbaugh and Stern followers, Reagan Democrats, white male academics, and the white men of the white supremacist movement. More importantly, white supremacist discourse functions to sustain a system of white, male, heterosexual privilege.

This convergence is also an example of the intricate ways in which race, gender, and class are intertwined. White men, as they choose to represent themselves in white supremacist discourse, identify quite explicitly along lines of gender and class, as well as race. With regard to gender, white men in these publications see themselves and their interests as gender bound, that is, as distinct from those of white women. In terms of class, white men envision affirmative-action programs as plots carried out by the state to maintain the class position of Jewish men and Jewish women while raising the class position of white women, Black men, and Black women at the expense of white men. And, most overtly, white supremacist discourse sets out race as a fundamental boundary between white men and both Blacks and Jews. Thus, white supremacist discourse, rather than being exclusively concerned with race and class, is at a basic level engaged in gender and sexual politics as well.

While visions of masculinity are central to white supremacist discourse, it is also possible to catch a glimpse of white femininity in the margins.

Glimpses of Femininity: White Women

Though less visible in white supremacist discourse than their counterparts, white women, like white men, occupy a particular space bounded by race, class, gender, and sexuality. Most often, they appear as markers of (white, hetero-) sexual attractiveness or as emblems of white motherhood. White women's particular position within a white supremacist discourse, both in the contemporary setting and historically, is a fusion of privilege and oppression.

There is a good deal of historical research that explores white women's status within white supremacist contexts both in the United States and abroad (Blee, 1991b; Hall, 1983; 1979; Hurtado, 1989; Koonz, 1987; Ware, 1992). White women have historically been—and continue to be—situated within a complex nexus of race, and often class, privilege combined with gender oppression. Images of white women, either as mothers or as sexual beings, are constructed in opposition to images of subordinated women, that is, to Black women. One example of this oppositional difference is evident in the dialectic of Black womanhood (Dill, 1983). This dialectic is based on the fact that Black women have historically been defined as workers in a world in which femininity is defined in terms of idleness. In such a context, it was only possible for white women to be defined in terms of idleness *because* Black women were defined in terms of work (Dill, 1983; 1984). This dualism is also evident in constructions of white women's sexuality and fertility. White women are portrayed within white supremacist ideologies as chaste, pure, asexual, good mothers, exemplars of femininity.

White women are represented within these publications in a manner consistent with these historical antecedents to contemporary white supremacist discourse. White women's gender and sexuality are the focus of these representations. On the one hand, white women are characterized as racial patriots: mothers reproducing for the white race, the personification of standards of beauty based on whiteness and the objects of white male sexual desire, feminized white racial warriors who are still, because of their beauty and reproductive abilities, in need of white male protection. On the other hand, these very qualities of sexual attractiveness and reproductive abilities make white women suspect as racial traitors.

White Women As Racial Patriots

White women are more than complicit in the white supremacist movement. White women are featured as members and organizers and have even been active in the violence. However, although white women may be members they are rarely, if ever, represented as leaders, or even ideal members, of the movement. White women are primarily valuable to the movement for two qualities: their reproductive abilities and sexual attractiveness. First, I want to address the issue of white women's value as reproducers of the white race.

Glorious White Motherhood

One of the primary areas of concern for white supremacists is the "declining white birthrate" *(NAAWP,* no. 20, 1982, p. 13 and throughout). This demographic reality symbolically threatens white cultural, economic, and political hegemony. White supremacists assume that if this trend can be reversed, white hegemony will be assured. It is not surprising then that white women's reproductive abilities are seen as crucial to the movement. For instance, one white woman is praised because she ". . . contributed eight beautiful, healthy children to the White race, and

Figure III.8

who could ask for more than that?" *(Racial Loyalty,* no. 38, 1987, p. 1).

The primary value of white women's reproductive abilities is further illustrated by an example from *NAAWP.* In a photo of a white woman and her child the symbolic value of white women as breeders is clear (fig. III.8). The banner above the photo reads, "Vanishing Breed?" and below the photo is a long caption, including the following:

> I love everything she represents and will come to be. In her I see the esthetic [*sic*] beauty of the West; the abiding, unselfish love of family, race, country and world. *(NAAWP,* no. 23, 1982, p. 3)

The implication here is that if this woman, and by extension every white woman, does not continue to "breed," then this "breed" and all that she represents will cease to exist. Much as the white woman a century ago was seen as the symbol of "the Southland," the personification of all that was good, so white women in this context represent the embodiment of all "the esthetic [*sic*] beauty of the West" (Hall, 1979).

While it may be unusual to find examples of such overt expressions of the value placed on white motherhood outside extremist white supremacist publications, it is not at all difficult to find evidence for the privileging of white motherhood within a broader cultural context. White women are portrayed within popular culture, for instance, as *essentially* maternal and as especially well-suited for rearing children. In the 1994 film *Grand Canyon,* for instance, the character "Claire" (portrayed by Mary McDonnell) resolves her own personal crisis in identity, prompted by her teenaged son's move away from the domestic sphere and her husband's distance in their marriage, by embracing motherhood. Rather than evaluate her life or present crisis with reference to the gender politics inherent in the "empty nest syndrome," the film has Claire reinvesting in those politics by adopting a child at a time when she is no longer able to have one physically. Claire's move to re-embrace motherhood serves, in part, to resolve issues surrounding racial politics raised by the film as well. The baby that Claire "discovers" (in true colonial fashion) is Hispanic and is therefore coded in the film as "not white." Claire finds the abandoned baby and eventually keeps it (in line with the "every thing happens for a purpose" theme of the film). This reifies the place of white motherhood as inherently "good" (she finds, "saves," and keeps the child) in juxtaposition to the position of "bad," racially Other motherhood (while the child's "not white" mother abandons it).

This representation of white women as the quintessential embodiment of "good" mothering pervades American popular culture. In another example, a television situation comedy, popular in the 1980s and now in syndication, "Webster," repeats the image by featuring a white mother (and father) and an adopted Black child. These images convey a representation of white women as inherently maternal, and as particularly well-suited for mothering, even when—or, perhaps, *especially* when—it comes to children who are "not white." Of course, there is a white patriarch overseeing the mothering (in both *Grand Canyon* and "Webster"), and the children are *adopted,* so as not to impugn the racial and sexual purity of the good, white mothers.

The white supremacist notion of glorious white motherhood depicted in extremist publications and reverberating throughout popular culture influences how we, collectively, interpret events. In 1994, in Union, South Carolina, Susan Smith, a young, white mother of two small children, reported that she had been carjacked and her children abducted by an unidentified Black man. The tale caused a nationwide search for the children and an outpouring of concern until Susan Smith confessed that she had rolled the car into a nearby lake with the children still inside. Smith's decision to implicate a Black man and her subsequent confession shattered much of the racial goodwill in Union (the search and concern had crossed racial boundaries). Most of the tension and discussion surrounding the case immediately afterward focused attention on the fact that our willingness to believe her story rested on an assumption that the culprit was a Black man; and, thus, the story worked because it appealed to cultural images of Black men as savage and criminal (as ontological suspects). While this is certainly true, it is also true, and little mentioned, that another reason so many of us believed Smith's story is that it just as effectively (and more surreptitiously) traded on cultural images of white motherhood. Just as it was plausible within a white supremacist context to believe that a Black man had attacked this white woman and abducted her children, it was just as implausible within that context to believe that this white woman, this "good" white mother, could have done harm to her children.

Objects of Sexual Desire

In addition to their value as "good" mothers and reproducers of the white race, white women are also valued within white supremacist discourse for their sexual attractiveness. As demonstrated in the quote accompanying the "Vanishing Breed?" illustration (see figure III.8), within white supremacist discourse white women signify "all that is beautiful."

The white supremacist strategy for highlighting white women's sexual attractiveness is to regularly contrast it with the alleged lesser attractiveness of Black women. For example, an article entitled "Blonde Models Are First" contends that the fashion industry agrees with white supremacists because "ads feature hundreds of blue-eyed blonde girls rather than 'mulattoes' " (*Thunderbolt*, no. 252, 1980, p. 11). In another example, the Miss America competition becomes the symbol of the white standard of beauty:

Miss America used to be the symbol of the exalted spiritual and sexual purity and chastity of the white woman, the envy of the world for

59

her beauty and fidelity to hearth and home. Then a mulatto named Vanessa Williams won the contest. . . . *(WAR,* vol. 4, no. l, 1985, p. 4)

Here, two standards of beauty are posited—one Black and one white—and, not surprisingly, it is the standard of white beauty which is affirmed.[7] White women's sexual attractiveness is symbolic of "exalted spiritual and sexual purity and chastity." This image of white women's sexuality as pure and chaste is strikingly similar to that implicit in the code of chivalry used to justify the practice of lynching (Carby, 1987b; Hall, 1983, 1979; Hurtado, 1989).

Diverging from this image of women as chaste, pure, and sexually attractive is the image of white women who are sexually attractive, but neither chaste nor pure. This more provocative sexuality is captured in an illustration regularly featured in *WAR* (fig. III.9). In this image a white woman appears nude from the waist up, carrying an automatic rifle. The caption reads, "My man is a white racist. If yours is a whimp [*sic*], dump him and get a real White man and screw the system" (*WAR,* vol. 6, no. 4, 1987, p. 9). Here again, white women are valued for their sexual attractiveness. In addition, the avenue of resistance to "the system" available to white women is through their sexuality, by "screwing" a "real White man."

Both images, the first of a sexuality that is chaste and pure, the second of a sexuality that is quasi-pornographic, emphasize the sexual attractiveness of white women. The split image of white women's sexuality is not as clear and simple a division as the classic Ma-donna/whore imag-ery, but it draws upon this trope to cat-egorize one type of woman as "good" and sexy, another as "bad" and sexy. Still, both categories of women

Figure III.9

are valued for their sexuality—a sexuality that is implicitly heterosexual and explicitly intended for the pleasure of white men.

The link between white supremacist images of white women as sexual objects within extremist publications and the broader white supremacist context in which white women occupy much the same space is fairly straightforward. The representation of white women—particularly young, thin, ingratiatingly heterosexual, women inevitably possessing long, blond hair—as the embodiment of "beauty" is ubiquitous in contemporary culture. Whether in fashion modeling, advertising, or mainstream pornography (like *Playboy* and *Penthouse)*, images of beauty and sexual attractiveness are inscribed on the body of a white woman—most popularly, an "all-American" type like Cheryl Tiegs or, more recently, Christie Brinkley; occasionally, brunettes, such as Cindy Crawford are fitted onto this cultural form; and rarely, a woman of color, like Naomi Campbell, may be incorporated. In some sense, then, the white supremacist publications cited above are correct: blonde models *are* first. The fashion industry, beauty pageants, and advertisers *do* prefer white women. The "white" lie in this instance, however, is that this preference—this privileging of white women within a white supremacist context—is *proof* of the superiority of white women, when it is naturally an elaborate justification for privilege based on race, class, gender, and sexuality in which middle- (and upper-) class, white, heterosexual women are viewed as somehow "better" than women designated as Others. Such reasoning exemplifies the kind of tautology, and the hegemony, of white supremacist discourse whether produced by extremists or by Madison Avenue.

The idealization of white women's beauty impacts all those who internalize such standards and yet feel they can never embody them. The prevalence of self-induced starvation (benignly referred to as "eating disorders") among young women in the United States is, in part, an attempt to conform to idealized standards of thinness, based on cultural representations of white, heterosexual women (e.g., Bordo, 1992; Thompson, 1993). And, cultural critic bell hooks reads pop icon Madonna's decision to dye her hair blonde as less a question of aesthetic choice than as an affirmation of "those characteristics that are seen as the quintessential markers of racial aesthetic superiority that perpetuate and uphold white supremacy" (1992:159). In this way, hooks contends, Madonna shares much in common with masses of Black women who "are forever terrorized by a standard of beauty they feel they can never truly embody" (1992:159). And, I would add, representations of white women as exemplars of beauty and sexual attractiveness in white supremacist publications share much in common with broader cultural representations of white women.

White women's value within white supremacist discourse derives from their reproductive capabilities as well as their sexual attractiveness and availability. These traits also insure that white women exist in a tenuous and subordinate position: either in need of protection or as potential traitors to the white supremacist cause.

White Women As Racial Warriors

The images of white feminine beauty and white motherhood come together in the image of the white woman warrior. This is a much rarer and more limited vision of "warrior" than the white male version. In fact, white women appear as warriors within only one issue of one publication, *WAR,* and their appearance is very restricted within this publication. *WAR,* unlike most other white supremacist organizations, briefly had a women's auxiliary, the Aryan Women's League (AWL). The AWL was founded in 1989 by "Monique Wolfing," a pseudonym, and had its own publication.[8] The AWL's purpose was to ". . . recruit White racially conscious women" to the white supremacist movement. In an article

Figure III.10

written in support of the AWL, "From a Man's Point of View," the author writes, "Our women are our auxiliary warriors to us, and we are damn proud of them" (*WAR,* vol. 8, no. 4, 1989, p. 14). It is in conjunction with this article in defense of the AWL that the only illustration of a white woman warrior appears (see figure III.10). This imagery of white women warriors, limited though it is, is important because it highlights the ambivalence surrounding the representation of white women within the publications.

In Need of Protection

A much more common portrayal than that of a white woman defending herself and her race is the depiction of white women in need of protection. As valuable reproducers of the white race and as sexual objects, white women are always portrayed as not safe and needing protection. Almost every issue includes at least one story of a white woman who has been attacked by a Black man.

Understood in this representation is the notion that white women are not capable of caring for themselves. Even in accounts in which a white woman can effectively protect herself, this ability is minimized. For instance, an article entitled "*Gun* Saves Girl From Terrorists" [emphasis mine] *(Thunderbolt,* no. 268, 1981, p. 8),

Figure III.11

reports the story of a white woman who fights off Black "beasts" in South Africa. Rather than highlight the woman's ability to defend herself, the incident is used to promote unrestricted gun ownership.

White women are viewed as in particular need of the protection of *white men*. White men are viewed as the rightful defenders of white women, children, and families. But from what, or from whom, is it necessary to protect white women? As alluded to already, white women are viewed as being in need of protection most frequently from Black male murderers and rapists. For instance, in an article called "Partly Paralyzed Veteran Dies Defending Wife," a white man heroically and tragically dies trying to defend his wife from a Black male intruder *(NAAWP,* no. 22, 1982, p. 7).

The threat to white women posed by Black men can also be seen in the accompanying illustration from *Racial Loyalty* (see figure III.11). In this image, a white woman answers her door only to be confronted by a menacing-looking Black man. The caption, supposedly being spoken by a white man, reads, "Advice of the Month: Never Open Your Door for Niggers" *(Racial Loyalty,* no. 71, 1991, p. 12). The message conveyed here is simple: white women are vulnerable to attack from Black men even in their own homes; white men must warn them, if not protect them, from this threat.

White women must be protected from more than Black men, however. White women must also be protected from "women's lib." For instance, in "The Real E.R.A," a writer for the *Torch* identified only as "Tamara Kintz" notes that the ERA would ". . . abolish all protective work laws for women, such as regulating heavy lifting" *(Torch,* vol. 12, no. 8, 1981, p. 7).

There is an ironic twist to white women's perceived need for protection and women's liberation. Apparently, white women are not seen as in need of protection from all aspects of gender equality, because even in nontraditional occupations, white women are defended. For example, "Army Women Harassed" details the story of a white woman who has to ". . . put up with the new racially mixed army." The article goes on to describe her experiences at the hands of a Black Army officer who ". . . sought to force his sexual desires on [a] young white woman" *(Thunderbolt,* no. 267, 1981, p. 4). In this incident the "need for protection" theme emerges once again, even on the job in nontraditional occupations. Perhaps it is *especially* white women in nontraditional occupations who are perceived as in need of the protection of white men.

Thus, white women are depicted in white supremacist discourse as valuable for their reproductive abilities and sexual attractiveness. And it is these same traits that are the basis for their portrayal as in need of protection. White women are not universally characterized as defenseless, because they are also, at least in a limited way, portrayed as racial warriors. However, the qualities of sexual attractiveness and reproductive capabilities that support the valorization of white women are easily transformed into weapons used against white women when they are suspected of being traitors to the white race.

White Women As Racial Traitors

White women occupy an ambivalent position within white supremacist discourse. While they are marginal members and occasional leaders within the movement, they are valued primarily for their reproductive abilities and their sexual attractiveness and availability to white men. However, unlike white men, white women are portrayed as potential traitors to the white race based on issues surrounding their reproductive abilities and sexual attractiveness.

White Women's Sexuality

White women are suspect as racial traitors because of their sexuality. White women are assumed to be vulnerable not only to sexual attacks by Black men, but also to sexual advances from Black men. White women are cautioned throughout these publications about the dangers inherent in associating with non-white men. An example of the repeated admonitions to white women appears in this illustration from *Racial Loyalty* (see figure III.12). In the drawing a Black man appears menacingly in the background, while the caption underneath reads, "White Women, don't let Jew run T.V. influence you or your daughters. Whites associate only with whites, and whites only marry whites" *(Racial Loyalty*, no. 66,

Figure III.12

1990, p. 12). Here again is the theme of white men as protectors, presumably a protective white man giving his advice to the white women in the illustration. Also evident here is the implicit assumption that white women are vulnerable to, and defenseless against, seduction by a Black man.

White women who do choose to have sex with Black men are vilified by white supremacist discourse, and the punishment for such behavior is severe. For instance, a cautionary tale of one such white woman who was killed by her Black boyfriend was printed in the *Thunderbolt* (*Thunderbolt*, no. 272, 1981, p. 7). The consequences of such treacherous behavior reach beyond white women. In another example, "Innocent Suffer from Mixed Couples," details the story of a white woman and her Black boyfriend who murdered the woman's family (*Thunderbolt*, no. 265, 1981, p. 5).

The potential threat of white women is taken seriously enough that some men in the movement search for white women they hope are less likely to be racial traitors. In order to assist white men in the search for a "life mate" who is less likely to be a racial traitor, *Racial Loyalty* offers "Cupid's Corner," a mail-order dating service that assists members in finding:

> an ideologically compatible life's partner . . . Objective: marriage and the founding of another white family. We are not interested in . . . merely the pen pal type of letter . . . nor those suggesting a live-in relationship. (*Racial Loyalty*, no. 8, 1984, p. 11)

The service appears to be a popular one because announcements of marriages which result from "Cupid's Corner" are a regular feature of *Racial Loyalty*.

White women are not only viewed as sexually attractive, but also as the sexual property of white men. White women are expected to be sexually available to white men. If they are not, then they are seen as traitors to their race. Thus, the sexuality of white women is, in all the issues analyzed to date, presumed to be heterosexuality. Although there are very few mentions of lesbians, none of the publications refer to lesbians as white women. The only lesbians featured in the texts are Jewish women or African American women. For example, *WAR* and other publications often describe leaders of the feminist movement as "bull dyke Jewess[es]" (*WAR*, vol. 4, no. 3, 1985, p. 10). Lesbians are represented as repulsive, disgusting, and "perverse." Presumably, the most repulsive women are women who are not available to white men. Theoretically, white lesbians are, because of their race, potential recruits for the white "resistance" movement, but because of their sexuality are denied entrée. This denial is based not only on a difference in "values," but on the grounds that white men do not have sexual access to these women.

Bearing "Non-White" Children

The penultimate affront to white men's control over white women's sexuality and reproductive lives is a white woman who chooses to not only have sex with, but also bear children with, a Black man. For instance, a controversial child custody case in which a white woman was initially denied custody of her white son from her first marriage because her second husband was a Black man made headlines in Louisiana. When the woman eventually won custody of her son, *NAAWP* ran a story about the case under the banner headline, "ABOMINATION: Race-Mixer Gets Custody" *(NAAWP,* no. 22, 1982, p. 6). Much of the rhetoric in the article focuses on her white son and the injustice done to him. The true target of the article is, however, the white woman who is vilified for being a "race-mixer."

Abortion

Abortion, according to white supremacists, is a form of racial treason when practiced by white women. Given the earlier description of the hallowed station of white motherhood as the highest calling and greatest contribution of white women within the movement, it is not surprising that abortion would be considered treason. The decline in white births, which is seen as directly tied to the decline of white hegemony, is attributed to the fact that fewer white women are willing to become pregnant. In addition, when white women do become pregnant some are inclined to terminate those pregnancies, or "murder their unborn children" *(Torch,* vol. 12, no. 8, 1981, p. l). The willingness of white women to abort white fetuses is juxtaposed with the image of Black and other minority women who are all too willing to conceive and bear "non-white" children (see figure III.13). A drawing from *Racial Loyalty* highlights this perceived disparity. In the illustration, a series of four panels, in each panel a woman of a different racial identity enters a clinic. In the first three panels, the women are all minority women, and each enters a clinic designated as a "Birth Clinic," while her numerous children wait outside. In the fourth panel, a white woman enters an "Abortion Clinic," and the doctor pictured says, "In a moment, we'll dispose of the child to be." The message is emphasized by the caption surrounding the panels, "Mud People Multiply! Whites Have Abortions" *(Racial Loyalty,* no. 59, 1990, p. 12).[9] Abortion, typically considered an issue of gender and sexuality, is in this context an essentially racial issue. And, it is white *women* who are the villainous perpetrators of this racial treason.

White women, then, occupy an ambivalent position within the movement. White women can be heroes and martyrs of the white "resistance" movement, just as white men can be. Yet they are restricted to a marginal status within the movement because of their potential reproductive and sexual betrayal of white men and the white racial movement. White women are thus simultaneously complicit in and held in contempt by the white resistance movement.

However, it would be missing the point of my argument to contend that white women are oppressed by their marginalization within this discourse. What I do intend to suggest is that the ways in which white women are depicted within this discourse can give us insight into the way in which race, class, gender, and sexuality are linked in the broader cultural context of white supremacy. Let me draw on another example from contemporary popular culture to illustrate what I mean.

Figure III.13

In Los Angeles in the summer of 1994, Nicole Brown Simpson and her friend, Ron Goldman, were murdered outside her condominium. O. J. Simpson,[10] the ex-husband of Nicole, was subsequently arrested and put on trial for the murders. In the months during the trial (and for long afterward), large segments of the population became enthralled by the case, and much of this fascination centered around Nicole and her life before she was killed. This intense interest in Nicole was in part based on the representations of white women in the white supremacist context which I have delineated here. Mainstream newspapers, supermarket tabloids, and network news broadcasts fostered a climate of debate about Nicole's character. On the one hand, she was portrayed as the "good" mother, emblematic of white womanhood, lovingly caring for her two children. Family photos and videotapes of Nicole in motherly embrace with her children and testimony of friends, family, and acquaintances supported

68

this view. On the other hand, allegations began to surface that Nicole was, in reality, a "slut" (or euphemistically, a "party girl") who would, during the time after her divorce, put her children down for the night and then go out to clubs dancing or have sex with men on the living-room sofa. The discussion of Nicole inevitably represented one of these two images (or highlighted both as the "two sides" of Nicole). And, as evidence emerged of Nicole's history of abuse at the hands of her ex-husband, so did questions about the nature and context of that abuse. Was she the "good" white mother, viciously abused and mistreated by her husband? Or, was she an uncontrollable "bad" girl, given to her own storms of rage and violent outbursts? Both portrayals of Nicole exist within a framework of idealized standards of white beauty, as her sexual attractiveness was inevitably mentioned in news reports, yet, rarely if ever did O. J. Simpson's first wife, a Black woman, get characterized as "attractive." White standards of sexual attractiveness are also predicated on the presumption of heterosexuality that prevails in the instance of Nicole, whose sexuality, in spite of revelations of a relationship with another woman, is always depicted as having been directed exclusively at men. Thus, the presentation of Nicole Brown Simpson in popular culture and the wide interest in the most intimate details of her life reflect core themes about white femininity contained in white supremacist discourse, whether in extremist publications or tabloid television.

The other aspects of the Simpson case—that Nicole's ex-husband and accused killer was O. J. Simpson, a successful, Black man; that this was an interracial relationship between a Black man and a white woman; and that their children are "mixed"—are all also part of the reason for the fascination with the case. And, the themes of race, class, gender, and sexuality inherent in the Simpson case go to the heart of white supremacist discourse and to the representations of Blacks within that discourse.

4

"Rapists," "Welfare Queens," and Vanessa Williams: Black Men and Black Women

White supremacist ideology is first and foremost about the degradation of Black bodies in order to control them.

—Cornel West, Race Matters, *1993*

Maintaining images of Black women as the Other provides ideological justification for race, gender, and class oppression.

—Patricia Hill Collins, Black Feminist Thought, *1990*

In the fall of 1994, two events marked the landscape of American politics and popular culture. Republicans swept the congressional elections and for the first time in several decades held a majority of legislative seats. The newly elected Speaker of the House, Newt Gingrich, rose to prominence on the national political scene in no small measure because of his call for welfare reform, taking the Democrats' similar proposal to a new level by advocating institutionalizing the children of single mothers relying on government assistance, inevitably referred to as "welfare mothers." Democrats as well as Republicans turned to authorities such as Charles Murray to shore up their attacks on poor women. Although both Democrats and Republicans were politically saavy enough to cast such concerns in racially neutral terms, the image of the "welfare mother" conjured in the minds of most Americans was of a young, Black woman. And it is an image that represents Black women (and by implication Black men) as sexually promiscuous and reproductively irre-

71

sponsible. It is an image not that far removed from extremist white supremacist discourse.

Competing with the congressional elections for network airtime (and
usually winning) was the O. J. Simpson trial. Americans, Black and white,
were riveted by the trial, and network news, mainstream newspapers, as
well as tabloid television and supermarket rags were filled with minutiae
of the court proceedings, the Simpsons' lives, and reports of any and
everyone with even the remotest connection to the case. Perceptions of
Simpson's guilt or innocence at the beginning of the trial revealed a wide
racial chasm, with 68 percent of whites believing Simpson was guilty, while
61 percent of Blacks believe he was innocent. The court battle over Simpson's guilt or innocence goes to the very heart of white supremacist notions of Black masculinity and white femininity, and the way we interpret
cultural events within the framework of these constructions. Is he the savage beast who committed these brutal crimes, set off by his uncontrollable
passion for a white woman? Or is he, as so many before him, an innocent
Black man entrapped by his involvement with a white woman and wrongly
accused by a white "justice" system? The public opinion polls seem to indicate that whites and Blacks have very different answers to these questions; and, in this instance at least, the opinion of a majority of white
Americans is consistent with the representations of Black masculinity in
extremist white supremacist discourse.

The connections between these two seemingly disparate events—congressional elections and the O. J. Simpson trial—lie in the intricate connections of race, class, gender, and sexuality. As the quotes by West and
Collins cited at the beginning of this chapter suggest, white supremacist
discourse (whether extremist or not) is concerned with degrading Black
bodies, specifically gendered and sexualized bodies, for the purpose of
justifying oppression. These images of race, gender, and sexuality which
resonate so effectively in political elections and popular culture are at
their most overt in white supremacist discourse.

"Blackness" in White Supremacist Discourse

Blacks are depicted by white supremacist discourse as the antithesis of
whites in every way. The rearticulation of "whiteness" depends in large
measure on the construction of distinct races which are *not* included in
the racial categorization "white" and the corresponding rhetorical subordination of those categories. This process relies on many of the themes
which have been prevalent in racist ideologies for centuries and which are
evident in contemporary white supremacist discourse. Perhaps most strik-

ing is that the catalog of basic "white supremacist propositions" which Frederickson (1983) delineates concerning the majority of whites in the United States in the 1830s still accurately describes the views of a tenacious minority at the end of the twentieth century.

These propositions, including biological notions of Black inferiority in every dimension, are further complicated by notions of gender and sexuality. Images of Black men and Black women within white supremacist publications are gender-specific portrayals constructed in relation to those of white men and white women. In this chapter, I examine images of Black men and Black women and the ways in which those racial images are constituted along lines of gender and sexuality. Before beginning this exploration it is useful to consider the construction of "Blackness" within white supremacist discourse.

Constructing "Blackness"

African Americans are not to be found within the publications, but "negroes," "niggers," and "Blacks" are. As with "whiteness," "Blackness" or who is "Black" is most often a taken-for-granted assumption. One simply is, or is not, Black. The image of "Blackness" and those placed in that category is determined by the same framers of discourse who construct the image of whiteness, that is, white men.

"Blackness" is perhaps most importantly defined as that which is "not white." This distinction is illustrated in an article featured in *The Klansman*. The article relates an incident at a Klan rally and cross-lighting ceremony in which

> a camouflage-clad Klansman brandishing an AR-l5 semiautomatic rifle approached WDVM reporter trainee Jocelyn Maminta and asked her to leave the rally site. "We don't allow blacks here," the armed Klansman said as Maminta and her cameraman were ushered toward their car. When another reporter responded that Maminta is not black, a robed Klansman replied, "She's not white." (*The Klansman*, no. 115–16, 1985, p. l)

Although the specific racial identity of the reporter is never established, it need not be because the significance here is that "she's not white."

The distinctiveness of those who are "not white" is further highlighted in an article in the *Torch* entitled "How to Deal with Niggers." It offers a numbered list of ten pieces of advice, including number nine: "Never forget that you are dealing with a basic savage and *while he may in some ways appear to be like you, he is not and never will be"* [emphasis mine] (*Torch*, vol. 12, no. 9, 1981, pp. 3, 5). The contradiction is striking; the initial reference to the "basic savage" nature of Blacks is called into question in the last half of the sentence which acknowledges the fundamental sameness of Blacks and whites as human beings. While whites may indeed see similarities between themselves and Blacks, the space that opens for resisting racial divisions or, at the very least, reconsidering the significance of race is closed with the admonition, "he is not and never will be" like the white reader.

Implied within these examples and laid out explicitly elsewhere is an essence of "Blackness" that is the opposite of "whiteness"; to be "not white" is constructed as an absence of "whiteness." The substance of "whiteness" and "Blackness" is explicated in *Racial Loyalty*, which regularly features lessons for readers on "Phrases and Words of Wisdom of the Classical Latin."[1] In one such lesson on "niger lapillus" and "albus lapillus," the author uses the following illustration:

> Ancient White Romans had a habit of marking a bad or unlucky day with a *black* pebble (*niger* lapillus), and a good or lucky day with a *white* pebble (*albus* lapillus). For ancient White Romans white color had a special, almost religious significance as a symbol of everything good, pure, beautiful, honorable, while black color was associated with everything bad, muddy, ugly, evil [emphasis in original]. (*Racial Loyalty*, no. 67, 1991, p. 11)

The dichotomy here between "Blackness" and "whiteness" is unmistakable. The "almost religious" white symbol stands for all that is good, while the essence of "Blackness" is associated with "everything bad, muddy, ugly, evil." Franz Fanon traced this symbolic split between the supposed purity and benevolence of whiteness and the Satanic image of the Black in Western culture and also provided evidence of the ways that these cultural archetypes were imbedded within the psychic structure of his white patients (1967). Fanon's point was that Western culture has imputed certain characteristics, "goodness" or "evil," to specific individuals based on their association with one side or the other of a symbolic dichotomy. The tautology of white supremacist discourse is that, as in the example cited here, the presence of this cultural dichotomy is taken as *prima facie* evidence of ascribed differences between racial groups.

White supremacist discourse embraces an essentialism that is biologically based. Most prominent within the discourse as physical markers are skin color, the shape of nose and lips, and hair texture. These physiognomic characteristics are taken as unimpeachable evidence of one's membership in a particular racial category. For example, in an article in *WAR*

Essentialist biology?)

discussing whether two "almost white" women who identify themselves as Black are in fact Black, the author points out that "they are obviously not Black-skinned or even dark-brown" but that they have "negroid features," such as "flaring, baboon nostrils . . . and swollen lips" (*WAR*, vol. 4, no. 1, 1985, p. 4). In another discussion about whether an individual is Black or not, the author cites the man's "dark skin and kinky hair" as evidence of his "negro blood" which is distinct from "white blood" (*Torch*, vol. 12, no. 8, 1981, p. 6). All the illustrations in the publications which feature Blacks emphasize exaggerated versions of these physical characteristics. Blacks are uniformly pictured with very dark skin, broad noses, enormous lips, protruding eyes, and "kinky" hair.

As further evidence of the biological basis and inherent inferiority of *illness* "Blackness," white supremacist discourse turns to the subject of illness. An issue of the *Thunderbolt* called the "Special 'Racial Differences' Edition," expounds on a plethora of Black biological infirmities. Just a few of the topics included are the "Physical Race Differences" of Black skin including "razor bumps" and vitiligo; "Causes of Negro Deaths," citing higher cancer rates for Blacks, along with "other causes of death includ[ing] heart/lung disease, chronic alcoholism, automobile and industrial accidents"; "Rapid Heartbeat in Black Babies," thought to be a predictor of high blood pressure, "which is twice as common among blacks as whites"; and "Sickle Cell Anemia—Negro Blood Disease" (*Thunderbolt*, no. 274, 1982, pp. 1–3, 8–9). Here again the lines between "good" and "bad," between white and Black, are evident in this discussion of illness. As Gilman has noted, "the very concept of pathology is a line drawn between the 'good' and the 'bad' " (1985:23). And very often, pathology is associated with race and with sexuality. Physical characteristics which become markers of racial difference, such as skin color, are also simultaneously associated with pathology and with sexuality (Gilman, 1985:25).

Whites' desire not to associate with Blacks is also attributed to biological differences. An article in the same issue of the *Thunderbolt* called "Real Cause of Body Odor," links ear wax and body odor. The study, purportedly conducted by a Japanese geneticist, finds:

> the world's three chief races have differences in ear wax . . . Orientals have dry wax and very low body odor. Whites have a wet wax and are subject to body odor. Negroes have an oily, sticky ear wax and strong repelling body odor . . . White people who have had to work alongside blacks [complained]. They have stated that black body odor is so repugnant that it is overpowering and can make White workers sick. It is a totally different smell than that emitted by White people. (*Thunderbolt*, no. 274, 1982, p. 3)

The biological basis of race is fixed here between three distinct groups, "Orientals," "Whites," and "Negroes." The article seeks to lend scientific credibility to the notion that Blacks have a body odor "so repugnant" that whites are overcome by it. The author lets no ambiguity remain by closing the article with the observation that it is a "totally different smell" than whites' body odor. Here again, discourse about essential, biologically based racial categories is conflated with that about pathology to lend a veneer of plausibility to a preposterous racial stereotype.

"Blackness" and its attendant biological inferiority is also seen as determinative of low intelligence. The special issue of the *Thunderbolt* includes a diagram of three skulls, a "Gorilla," a "Negro," and a "Whiteman," with the information "Skull angle gives Whites larger forebrain where intelligence cells are found" (*Thunderbolt*, no. 274, 1982, pp. 8–9). Accompanying the diagram is an article called "Inferiority of the Negro Brain," which further explains the connection between skull angle, brain structure, and intelligence:

> The negro brain is structured differently with less fissures and less complex cortex of the brain which indicates a lowered intelligence. [Therefore] . . . overall functional ability of the brain is reduced. (*Thunderbolt*, no. 274, 1982, p. 9)

This article articulates an unquestioning belief in the biological basis of intelligence and argues for the lower intelligence of Blacks on that basis. The final evidence offered here in the case for low levels of Black intelligence is presented in a chart titled, "Negro I.Q. Lower than Whites," in which Blacks in every state represented had significantly lower I.Q. scores than whites (*Thunderbolt*, no. 274, 1982, p. 9).

For those who may have still missed the message about Blacks' alleged biologically based inferiority, *WAR* offers the following illustration under the title, "Let's Answer the Scientific Question . . . What's on a Nigger's Mind?" [title and text not included here] (see figure IV.1). The text next to the illustration follows the theme of lending scientific credibility to theories of Black intellectual ability and reads:

> Research reveals that the Negro brain has shown considerable advancement since his crude jungle origin . . . the major significant change reflects his astounding ability to adapt to the relatively new environment of North America . . . today, with the advent of more opportunities to commit crimes, the organ's capacity for criminal behavior has nearly doubled! (*WAR*, vol. 8, nos. 5 and 6, 1989, p. 5)

76

Then the diagram points to different segments of the brain, one of the smallest of which is labeled "intelligence."

White supremacist assertions of the allegedly racially based lower intelligence of Blacks are not limited to extremist publications, however, but also appear under the guise of social science research. In the fall of 1994, Charles Murray and Richard Hernstein, fully credentialed academic social science researchers, published *The Bell Curve*, in which they argued that I.Q. is largely attributable to genetic heritage and that Blacks as a group are less intelligent than whites. The authors also suggest that if low I.Q. scores are related to poverty (as

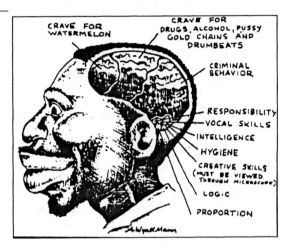

Figure IV.1

they believe they are), then whites and Blacks alike should accept the reality of Black intellectual disadvantage.

The connection between this widely discussed social science research and extremist white supremacist discourse is not a difficult one to make. First, despite Murray's [and while he was alive, Hernstein's—he died just as the book was released] vehement denials of harboring racist sentiment, the discussion presented in *The Bell Curve* of race and I.Q. bluntly sanctions white supremacist notions about the biological inferiority of Blacks, albeit in much more sophisticated language than the extremist publications. That Hernstein and Murray inundate the reader with an avalanche of charts, graphs, and statistics to substantiate their point makes it no less an artifact of white supremacist ideology; it merely demonstrates that white supremacy can take on a particularly pernicious form when it appears as social science.

Second, there is a more direct link to white supremacist sources in Murray and Hernstein's work. When interviewed by *The New York Times*, Murray conceded that part of what he found compelling about researching I.Q. and race was that it had the "allure of the forbidden," and that he and Hernstein were aware of this. "Some of the things we read to do this work, we literally

77

hide when we're on planes and trains. We're furtively peering at this stuff" (*New York Times*, October 9, 1994, p. 51). Intrigued by what these publications might be, Charles Lane in an article for the *New York Review of Books* finds that much of the research for *The Bell Curve* draws on the overtly racist journal *The Mankind Quarterly* and on the work of avowedly racist "scholars" who regularly contribute to *Mankind*. While Lane contends that Murray and Hernstein should not be held accountable for the views of all the researchers upon whose work they draw, he does argue convincingly that the use of these sources raises serious questions of intellectual honesty. In the interview with the *New York Times*, Murray conceded that he and a group of friends had, as teenagers in Iowa, burned a cross made of scrap wood on a hillside. The teenagers were surprised when their prank was interpreted as racial harassment of the two Black families in the town. When asked about the incident, Murray remarked, ". . . it never crossed our minds that this had any larger significance. And I look back on that and say, 'How on earth could we be so oblivious?'" (p. 52). Indeed. As an adult, Murray continues to ignite incendiary racial issues—here, the notion of Black inferiority—and chooses to remain willfully oblivious of any larger significance.

The current furor over Murray and Hernstein's work is reminiscent of the 1969 debate which ensued over William Shockley's work. A Nobel Prize–winning physicist, Shockley argued, just as Murray and Hernstein do, that Blacks are genetically less intelligent than whites. Shockley was widely heralded in white supremacist publications as an apologist for movement ideology, and references to him appear throughout the publications. Since Murray and Hernstein's work came out after the data was collected for this study, I can only speculate on the wide praise their work must have received within white supremacist publications.

For all the biological markers of Blackness (and its attendant inferiority) within white supremacist discourse, it is not always precisely clear who belongs in the category Black. Distinctions between the essence of "blackness" and "whiteness" are crystallized in discourse involving "mulattos," the term used for those of a "mixed" racial heritage. An example comes from an article in the *Torch* called "Fact, not Hate," concerning Alexandre Dumas, son of a French aristocrat and Haitian slave woman, and author of *The Three Musketeers* and *Count of Monte Cristo*. The article takes issue with the praise Dumas's work has received, especially when that praise is used as evidence in an argument for racial equality. The article debates whether Dumas is Black or white and considers what should be made of the genius attributed to his work. This is what follows:

> True, according to a racist[2] standard we would consider Dumas Black. Yet, his greatness, if any should be attributed to his White an-

cestors and not to his tree-swinging forbearers from Africa. . . . On the same subject dealing with so-called Black men who are more racially White (as Dumas was), than Black . . . When we try to discuss the natural abilities of the NEGRO, the liberals, Reds and Jews instantly start pointing with pride to creatures which are *anything but real Negroes*—men who are always almost WHITE *men with a small amount of Negro blood in them*. . . . If you wish to know the properties of the Negro, you must examine him ALL BY HIMSELF, the way he comes out of the Congo. When we do this we find not . . . intelligence and abilities . . . but something far more akin to the African gorilla—something dark and terrible, something animal-like and primitive. That is not "Hate"; that is a FACT [emphasis in the original]. (*Torch*, vol. 12, no. 8, 1981, p. 6)

The contention here is that Dumas is "anything but a real Negro"; indeed, he is "more racially White than Black" because he has only a "small amount of Negro blood." Thus, Dumas's achievement must be attributed to his White ancestors. In this instance of a man of racially ambiguous status, the decision about whether he is Black or white remains unsettled. What remains clear, however, is that anything worthwhile he accomplishes can be attributed to "whiteness" rather than any "Blackness" that may linger.

The issue of people of racially "mixed" heritage is a vexing one within white supremacist discourse. This is evident in an article from *WAR* which addresses this issue directly, called "Whatever Happened to the Word Mulatto?" In this article, the author laments the passing of such a useful term and attributes its current disfavor to the advent of Orwellian "newspeak" promoted by "Big Brother." In the following passage, Big Brother embraces a racial agenda as he tries to promote Vanessa Williams and Suzette Charles[3] as "Black" women:

Big Brother may describe them as Black, but they are obviously not Black-skinned or even dark-brown. They are lightly coffee-colored, almost White. They have mostly White features, except for flaring, baboon nostrils . . . and swollen lips . . . This is the way the Establishment has of pawning Black power and Black integration on us by . . . trotting out a 4/5's White woman who's 1/5 Black and calling her "Black." (*WAR*, vol. 4, no. 1, 1985, p. 4)

Here again, the notion of "Blackness" is a fixed one. Indeed, "Blackness" is so tangible a substance that individuals can have measurable percentages of this essence within them.

Even when racial identity is firmly established it can be transformed through sexual intercourse. Included in the "special issue" of the *Thunderbolt* is an article based on a "classified medical report marked 'RESTRICTED' published by Applied Trophology" in August 1959, which in 1982 had "just now reached this editor." A portion of the article, described as a "shocking revelation," reads as follows:

> Some scientists now even believe that without impregnation, sexual intercourse with a black male leads to an infusion of the black sperm into the system of the White female which affects her body chemistry toward negroidal traits. Thus, in effect a White woman who engaged in sex with negroes should be considered no longer to be a part of the White Race. She has actually become part of a "race change." We believe that such activity can even cause mental changes in the White female which would tend to make her pro-negro and pro-race mixing because she has in a chemical way become part of the black race even though she still has the appearance of a White person. (*Thunderbolt*, no. 274, 1982, p. 9)

Race, in this passage, is a permeable category, one that even if fixed by all the biological determinatives set out earlier can still be altered by sexual contact. Specifically, it is the "infusion of black sperm" into a white woman that results in a change in "body chemistry toward negroidal traits." That such white women should not be "a part of the White Race," illustrates once again the image of white heterosexual women as racial traitors when they have sex with Black men (discussed in chapter 3). The infectious quality attributed to "black sperm" highlights the way notions of pollution, pathology, race, and sexuality are conflated within white supremacist discourse. It is no coincidence that "Blackness" here is transferred from Black men to white women, because within white supremacist discourse "Blackness," or what it means to be "Black," is most often equated with Black men.

Black Men

Blacks, like whites, are not regarded as ungendered. Rather, it is Black men who are most frequently featured as the embodiment of the dark Other in white supremacist discourse.

Black men are represented in ways that are unique and distinguishable from depictions of men of other racial groups or Black women. The portrait painted of Black men is, almost without exception, that of the Black man as "threat." Black men are seen as threats to the white social order in a series of arenas: as criminals, as economic and political threats, and in terms of their sexuality.

"Blackness," within white supremacist discourse, is most often situated in the body of a Black man (see figure IV.2). In this caricature of a Black man, he is shown beneath the caption "Today's Young Coon," indicating that he is typical of all young Black men. He stands near a jam box, holding a smoking gun in his right hand, and grabbing his sizable crotch with his left hand. He appears disheveled and unclean, as flies circle his head. Making the explicit message of the drawing still more overt, the text in the sidebar accompanying the drawing (not included here) describes the man as:

Figure IV.2

crude, smelly, loud, uneducated, inarticulate and preoccupied with the most base and petty endeavors. . . . He's very committed to his music . . . which shamelessly promotes violent revolution, irresponsible sexuality and the mindless worship of trinkets and trends. (*WAR*, vol. 8, no. 2, 1989, p. 11)

The text and the drawing create an image of Black men as beasts, a bestiality located in the body. That the man stands slouched, grabbing his crotch, indicates that he is centrally concerned with the body, and most importantly his penis. Indeed, as Fanon noted in his analysis of white psychiatric patients, "One is no longer aware of the Negro, but only of a penis: the Negro is eclipsed. He is turned into a penis. He *is* the penis" (1970:120). Here, the Black man who is "preoccupied with the most base and petty endeavors" and listens to a music which promotes "irresponsible sexuality" is eclipsed, he *is* the penis.

The threat of political power implicit in this imagery should not be overlooked. In his other hand, the Black man holds a gun that appears to have been recently fired (at whites?). The text refers to the music which "shamelessly promotes violent revolution." The association of the phallic gun and the reference to "violent revolution" points to the real fear that underlies much of this discourse. While large segments of the Black population continue to be politically and economically disenfranchised, and among the least powerful members of our society, it is these people that white supremacists fear. The thought that Blacks, especially young Black men, could arm themselves and foment a "violent revolution" is a fear that is deeply ingrained in white supremacist ideology and in more mainstream reports of "fear of crime." Both are linked in the white imagination to images like this one of Black man-as-penis, Black man-as-animal. The fear is that Black men will shift the focus of their rage away from each other and toward whites. The irony of this type of projection, of course, is that it is white supremacists who are advocating a violent revolution. In addition, the implication of the drawing elides the fact that young Black men are statistically much more likely to harm each other than whites. And, further, projecting the possibility of "violence" against whites onto young Black men distorts the reality that for centuries violence by whites against Black men (and women) has been institutionalized whether historically in slavery, sharecropping peonage, Jim Crow segregation, and lynching, or currently in *de facto* segregation coupled with economic and political disenfranchisement.

This drawing further illustrates the centrality of the body to the construction of racist discourse. Indeed, in this instance, the body of a Black man furnishes the "metaphorical medium for distinguishing the pure from the impure, the diseased from the clean and acceptable, the included from the excluded" (Goldberg, 1990:305). This Black man's body signifies all that is impure, diseased, and excluded in white supremacist discourse. The juxtaposition of the white men discussed in the previous chapter and the Black man in this drawing highlights the contrasting images of white and Black masculinities and the centrality of the body to each.

Criminal Black Men

Crime is emblematic of the rearticulation of "whiteness" and its concurrent recasting along lines of gender and sexuality. Within the mainstream news media, crime reports typically feature white victims of Black perpetrators and virtually never address the issue of "race." While some may applaud such a "color-blind" approach, the vacuum left in the absence of any kind of analysis (and within the broader social context of white supremacy discussed in chapter 2) reifies the messages inscribed in the images of white victims and Black perpetrators replayed again and again on the evening news. Such reports have become thinly veiled codes for whites' (both men and women) fear of young, Black men who are continually presumed to be criminals. The impact of such reports is heightened even further when a white woman is the victim of a crime at the hands of a young, Black man, or a group of young, Black men, as in the case of the Central Park jogger.

The reality, as is so often the case with white supremacist ideology, is just the opposite. Although it is whites who complain more vocally about crime and are seen as more shaken as victims of crime, it is, in fact, Blacks who have a much greater likelihood of becoming victims of crimes than whites (Hacker, 1992:191). This reinterpretation of crime, an issue which affects all of us, as a *racial* issue, that is, one of Black perpetrators and white victims, is the essence of rearticulating whiteness; this whiteness is simultaneously reinterpreted along lines of gender and sexuality.

Whether in mainstream news reports or in white supremacist publications, Black men are represented as criminals. This construction rests fundamentally on a biological notion of Black masculinity as inherently volatile, explosive, and dangerous. In white supremacist literature, Black men are represented as a particular type of criminal: especially vicious thugs inclined toward rapacious, murderous attacks against whites.

The criminality of Black men is a constant theme in the publications and can be illustrated in a variety of ways. All of the publications include at least one page that features "crime news." Although the length of the stories and the amount of editorial comment may vary, the theme—Black men assaulting white women, white men, and white families—does not. For example, most issues of *NAAWP* include "crime news." They simply reprint articles from mainstream newspapers (without permission or citation) without editorial comment. The *Thunderbolt* routinely carries news stories under the banner, "News Media Suppresses News on 'Missing and Murdered' Whites." One such story included the subheading, "Nation-Wide Black Crime Wave," in which readers are informed:

violent murders have reached an all time high in many American cities with negroes being the killers in over 85% of the cases . . . The press and TV are covering up the killings of Whites by blacks in order to make the crime wave look like a onesided affair in which only blacks are suffering. (*Thunderbolt*, no. 26f, 1981, p. 1)

The first three pages of this issue are filled with story after story of crimes all committed by Black males.

As expected, the criminality of Black men is argued to have a biological foundation. In the illustration from *WAR* featured above, one of the largest brain segments is labeled "criminal behavior" (see figure IV.1). A series of articles featured in the *Thunderbolt*'s crime pages illustrates this point in an only slightly more subtle manner. Under a two-page banner that reads, "Negroes Committing Over 90% of Violent Crime in Big Cities," photos of four Black men, all brothers, are featured. The caption beside the photo declares, "They're insanely vicious and sadistic thugs . . . who have committed as many as 6,000 violent crimes. . . ." Two other articles under the same banner report similar stories of brothers in crime, "Two Brothers Guilty of 132 Felonies," and "Seven Brothers Ar-

rested 192 Times," further suggesting a biological basis of Black male crime (*Thunderbolt*, no. 259, 1980, pp. 6–7).

The criminality of Black men is not only seen as innate, it is also characterized as particularly savage, even animalistic. Black male attackers in accounts of crime news are often described using adjectives which indicate they are something less than human. They are described as "bestial," "savage," or "animalistic," as in the admonition, "never forget

Figure IV.3

that you are dealing with a basic savage . . ." (*Torch*, vol. 12, no. 9, 1981, pp. 3, 5). The notion of Black male savagery is clearly evident in this illustration from *WAR* (see figure IV.3). Two black men appear in the drawing, one in street clothes, the other in a loincloth, and the inscription ponders whether gang violence is "just good old-fashioned Tribal Warfare" and warns that Black men will "turn your cities into jungles" (*WAR*, vol. 8, no. 2, 1989, p. 10). The implication here is that not only are Black men inherently savage, but also that their savage nature is a powerful force which will transmogrify cities into "jungles" unless white people "wake up."

The danger allegedly posed by Black men is explored in great depth in an article from the *Torch* entitled "White Prisoner in a Black Prison," by Fred T. Durrough, a white inmate, who writes:

> Niggers are for the most part harmless in jail when you have only one or two in a tank where they are outnumbered by whites. Like most *animals* they only attack when they are sure of an easy victory. *Like* the *jackel* [*sic*], they *lay back while the lion eats and only attempt to steal the food when their numbers become large.* . . . black savages hate whites and want to get the upper hand [emphasis added]. (*Torch*, vol. 12, no. 9, 1981, p. 3)

Here the themes of Black men as criminals and Black men as less than human converge. Black men are likened to "animals," specifically "jackels [*sic*]," who "steal their food."

Black men are assumed to be criminal not only because of their inherent criminal nature, but also because they are too lazy to work. This is illustrated in the following drawing from *Racial Loyalty* (see figure IV.4). A Black man is portrayed as

GET YA LAZY BUTT OUT OF THAT BED WOMAN...WE GOT WHITE FOLKS TA ROB, AND DRUGS TA BUY.

Figure IV.4

too lazy[4] "ta rob" the "white folks" he must in order to buy drugs (*Racial Loyalty*, no. 44, 1988, p. 12).

The image of Black men as criminal resonates so effectively that several of the publishers use this image as a regular feature. An issue of *NAAWP* uses a photograph of a Black man pointing a gun at a white man. The caption underneath reads, "Will you let him pull the trigger and destroy our future and the beauty of our people, as illustrated above? Join the NAAWP and the white fight!" (*NAAWP*, no. 32, 1984, p. 3). Each issue of *Racial Loyalty* after September 1989 features a column on the front page entitled "Another Victim." Under the headline is a photo, typically of a white woman, who been assaulted or murdered by a "mud" person, most often a Black man. The caption under the man's picture reads, "The Face of the Racial Enemy."

Economic and Political Threats

Black men are also featured in the publications as direct economic threats to white men, primarily in the labor force. Figure IV.5 illustrates this point, as a Black man is welcomed into the employment office while the white man is booted out. According to these publications, this is indicative of the treatment Black men and white men commonly receive in employment offices across the United States.

Black men are an economic threat only tangentially to white women. Nowhere in the publications are Black men represented as taking jobs away from white women. This is in keeping with the publications' focus on white men as victims of affirmative action, while ignoring the benefits of affirmative action to white women. Black men are only portrayed as an economic threat to white women inasmuch as they interfere with white men's ability to provide economically for white families.

When Black men are depicted as a danger to white women in the labor force, that threat is both

Figure IV.5

economic and sexual. For instance, "Army Women Harassed" details the story of a white woman who has to ". . . put up with the new racially mixed army." The article goes on to describe her experiences at the hands of a Black Army officer who ". . . sought to force his sexual desires on [a] young white woman" (*Thunderbolt,* no. 267, 1981, p. 4).

The illustration featured here is also indicative of this theme (see figure IV.6). This cautionary cartoon from *Racial Loyalty* depicts a white woman face-to-face with a Black man, and the caption reads "Nigger Intimidation in the Work Force" (*Racial Loyalty,* no. 60, 1990, p. 12). The implication is that an integrated work force and the economic participation of white women leads inevitably to Black men's sexual advances which are made at the economic peril of white women.

Linked to the economic threat of Black men and yet potentially even more menacing is the Black man in politics. Black men who have succeeded economically may succeed politically, and this is perceived within the discourse as an imminent possibility with perilous consequences. While it is Blacks as a category who are perceived as politically threatening, it is Black *men,* specifically, who are seen as the manifestation of this threat and who are the primary targets of white supremacist rhetoric. For instance, the *NAAWP* featured an article titled "Black Mayors are Growing in Number in the U.S."(*NAAWP,* no. 31, 1984, p. 5).

Figure IV.6

The *Thunderbolt* has run articles such as "Georgia Gov. Promotes Black Power" (*Thunderbolt,* no. 232, 1978, p. 2) and "Black Revolution Threatened" (*Thunderbolt,* no. 248, 1979, p. 14). And, the *Torch* ran a story with the headline, "Negro City Official Threatens Warfare Against Whites" (*Torch,* no. 136, 1990, p. 8). These headlines imply a menacing Black threat to the established, white, political order, a threat that is embodied in Black men such as Marion Barry.

A profile of "Negro Politicians" in *The Klansman* included a story on the mayor of Washington, D.C.[5] Barry is described as a "typical negro male" who:

> In his official capacity . . . is pushing through a new law to LOWER the age of consent and to LEGALIZE homosexuality and sodomy! (*The Klansman*, no. 71, 1981, p. 5)

The article goes on to define terms such as sodomy for the uninitiated reader. Here, the threat that Black men in political power pose is not only to the established political order, but also to the established regulation of sexuality.

Much more subtly, the front page of an issue of *NAAWP* features a photo of a smiling James Meredith with the caption, "Integrationist Turned Segregationist." Meredith is described as being opposed to many of the things that the *NAAWP* stands for, yet he is held up for admiration because he "speaks his heart and mind so honestly" (*NAAWP*, no. 26, 1983, p. 1). Meredith, pessimistic about the possibility of Blacks achieving racial equality in the United States, is an advocate of the repatriation of African Americans to Africa. Meredith is praised by the *NAAWP* because "his unabashed honesty and efforts must evoke respect from racially aware Whites, for we would wish our political leaders were only half as forthright for Whites' interest as Meredith is for Blacks" (*NAAWP*, no. 26, 1983, p. 1). The picture painted of this particular Black man, then, is one of honesty, forthrightness, and political astuteness. Because Meredith's political aims coincide with those of the NAAWP, he is heralded as an exception to the masses of Black men.

Nevertheless, Meredith is the exception that proves the white supremacist rule that Black men are a serious threat to whites. Even in this uncharacteristically glowing portrait of Meredith there are clear indications that this Black man too is a political menace. The article features an interview in which Meredith is asked how his thinking has changed since he integrated the University of Mississippi. The interview continues:

> MEREDITH: Well, it's always been the same. My principal objective has always been to make me and my kind the dominant force in the world.
>
> NAAWP: How can that best be accomplished?
>
> MEREDITH: By reuniting the Black race.
>
> NAAWP: What do you mean by dominant?

MEREDITH: That means the dominant race.

NAAWP: How do you define that?

MEREDITH: I don't know but one way to define it. You dominate. You control others.

NAAWP: You think then that you should control the other peoples of the world?

MEREDITH: I think that this is ultimately what it has to go back around to.

The message conveyed here in Meredith's own words is of an impending political threat. The words of a Black man whose political vision is the domination of whites is the embodiment of white supremacists' fears. The juxtaposition in this article of praise for Meredith's honesty with his political views (which are, to say the least, not typical of African Americans) is a subtle, sophisticated, and effective way of packaging the same message about the political threat of Black men, which other publications do in a much cruder manner.

Yet there is some ambivalence in the way the economic and political threat of Black men is delineated within the publications. On the one hand, as we have just seen, Black men are menacing, potentially powerful economic and political rivals. On the other hand, Black men are also depicted as incompetent in both business and politics. For example, in an article called "Incompetency Bankrupts Negro Businesses," programs designed to increase the number of Black-owned businesses are criticized. The article reads:

> Black capitalism was the plan . . . to put blacks in private business. Special Loans were made available for new black owned companies. The result has been bankrupt firms, misspent money, and wasted tax dollars. (*Thunderbolt*, no. 271, 1981, p. 7)

The reason for this legacy of failed Black-owned businesses is "blacks have never been qualified on any large scale to operate complicated or technical businesses" (*Thunderbolt*, no. 271, 1981, p. 7). The rest of this page is filled with numerous articles detailing a host of Black-owned banks, stock brokerages, publications, and hair-care companies which have had financial difficulties.

Black men are no more adept at politics, according to white supremacist discourse. A series of articles under the banner, "Sorry Record of Black Officials," provides documentation of the political incompetence of

Black men (*Thunderbolt*, no. 271, 1981, p. 7). The headline is followed by photos of ten different black men accompanying assorted stories of fraud, bribery, kickbacks, embezzlement, scandals. In a similarly arranged series of articles, the banner this time reads, "U.S. Justice System Being Wrecked by Black Appointed Judges," and below it is a series of five short articles about "incompetent" Black judges, along with photos of five Black men. The article informs the reader "law and order breaks down under Black judges" (*Thunderbolt*, no. 285, 1983, p. 4).

The implications of "incompetent" Black men with political power are detailed in "Negro Incompetence Stymies Case." The article, published during the time period of the Atlanta child murders, lists a number of Black men in positions of power in Atlanta and attributes the slow progress in the case to the number of Black men working in law enforcement. Then, the article goes on to fully explain the danger inherent in Black men's political power:

> Ever since the black power element took over Atlanta's police and FBI agencies, their enforcement, morale, and effectiveness have hit rock bottom. When Blacks take power in any city, crime begins to rage out of control. Black officials disgracefully fight and slander one another and government breaks down. People have forgotten the drunken orgies which took place in the Georgia state capitol when negroes dominated it after the Civil War during the first Reconstruction. Today, we are living under the very same conditions in this Second Reconstruction. History has turned full circle once again. (*Thunderbolt*, no. 261, 1981, p. 2)

In this passage, it is clear that civilization itself cannot be sustained with Black men in political power; indeed, such a situation is tantamount to the anarchy and "drunken orgies" which allegedly took place during Reconstruction, and are impending in the "Second Reconstruction."

What these representations share is a complicated interweaving of notions about Black men. Ideas about Black men's criminality are conflated with ideas about "Blackness" as inherently "bad, ugly, evil," mixed with assumptions of low intelligence and incompetency to conclude that Black men are innately unfit to hold public office or any positions of power.

Black Men As Sexual Threats

In the publications, the sexual threat posed by Black men is ubiquitous. Black men are depicted as inherently and unalterably sexually aggressive.

90

Black male sexuality supposedly develops at an early age. A public school-teacher, writing in *NAAWP*, relates, "In talking to my many students, I learned that Black males become sexually active at age eleven" (*NAAWP*, no. 49, 1987, p. 3).

The sexual threat that Black men pose is also embedded in references to "breeding," another common theme in white supremacist discourse. *"breeding"* There is, for white supremacists, a direct, causal link between rampant, unrestrained Black sexuality and increases in the Black population. Statistics which project an increase in the proportion of the population composed of minority group members are featured in the publications along with foreboding portrayals of Black male sexuality. White supremacists view this excessive sexuality as so dangerous that dire punishment is required. One example of the extreme measures advocated to curb Black male sexuality is featured in *WAR*:

> These Blacks and other non-white promiscuous perverts are responsible for filling the land with the unwanted and they should be castrated without pity. (*WAR*, vol. 4, no. 4, 1985, p. 3)

Clearly, it's the sexuality of Black men, along with "other non-white" men, which is to blame for "filling the land" with non-white children. The solution to the perceived problem is to curb the sexuality of Black men by castrating them "without pity."

Characteristically, the *NAAWP* conveys a similar message in a less overt way. The *NAAWP* featured a story of a judge who was suspended without pay for ordering a black man with seven children to be sterilized (*NAAWP*, no. 26, 1983, p. 13). The story is printed without editorial comment, but the message is clear: the judge is being rational in his attempt to control the otherwise unchecked sexuality of this Black man and is being punished unfairly for this action.

The target of Black male sexual aggression is depicted as primarily, although not exclusively, white women. From *The Klansman*, "A Black man's dream is to make it with a White woman. Unfortunately, statistics show the majority of them get their dream. If not through willing methods they result [*sic*] to rape" (*The Klansman*, no. 131, 1987, p. 9). According to this passage, there is no higher aspiration for Black men than to "make it," that is, have sexual intercourse with a white woman. In fact, this drive is so compelling for Black men that they will seek to accomplish this goal through violent means if necessary.

The image of the sexually predatory Black man is also evident in this illustration from *WAR* (see figure IV.7). In this image, a Black man walks past a white woman on the street and leers at her as he passes (*WAR*, vol.

8, no. 2, 1989, p. 11). The caption suggests that this is the quintessential Black man. White women are not the only victims of Black men's untamed sexuality, however.

Black men are depicted as sexual attackers of white men as well. Most often, this is reported to occur in prison, for instance in this reference in an article from a white prisoner, who asks, "How many times have you read about the murders and rapes of white inmates in a jail cell?" Answering his own question, the author replies, "In 95% of these cases the victim was white and the rapists were black" (*Torch*, vol. 12, no. 9, 1981, p. 3). One article on the subject, titled "Prison Rape a National Scandal," even attempts to quantify the problem, stating:

Figure IV.7

> Either for perverted sexual gratification or out of pure hate for Whites, blacks continuously attack and rape White prisoners throughout the nation. . . . In Alameda County Calif., the situation is so bad that Whites are raped at the rate of 14 a night. (*Thunderbolt*, no. 261, 1981, p. 9)

Although the author in this case is not certain of the motivation of the rape of white men by Black men, he is certain that it is a pervasive problem.

Yet another contribution from a white inmate appeared under the heading, "Unbelievable Prison Horror." While this author offers no guess on the number of rapes which occur, or what motivation can be attributed to the rapists, he is adamant about the affect on white masculinity. His letter reads:

I am a white male inmate . . . I was not gay and still consider myself straight. But I am used like a female. I was raped by three blacks when I first arrived. . . . After the rape I was considered a "punk, fag, bitch" and referred to as "her, she, and it." I was stripped of my manhood . . . I've seen Whites beaten, stuck with homemade knives trying to keep their manhood by fighting off negro homosexual attacks. Some Whites submit and become gays because it is easier than to fight. All the White guys have blacks for their man . . . I am half a man now . . . (*Thunderbolt*, no. 255, 1980, p. 7)

Black male sexuality in this letter, as throughout the publications, is a direct threat to white masculinity. Black male sexuality is constructed as a dangerous, powerful, and uncivilized force that is hazardous to white women and a serious threat to white men.

As crude as these images—and the discourse surrounding them—are, strikingly similar ones surface in mainstream politics and in popular culture with very real consequences for the lives of Black men in the United States.

The American public's fascination, some might say obsession, with the O. J. Simpson trial is just one example. Simpson, although acquitted, continues to embody white supremacist archetypes of Black men as "beasts," ontologically violent, dangerous, and criminal. Prior to his arrest, O. J. Simpson represented a reassuring image—handsome, successful, easygoing—a counterpoint to the ominous stereotype, amid a cultural context in which discussion about the crisis of the Black man (a major exhibit at the Whitney Museum in 1994, *New York Times* articles, and talk-radio discussions) borders on the cliché. Simpson, like Bill Cosby (or his television alter ego, Heathcliff Huxtable), provided America with a heartening example of a Black man who had made it, who had reached the pinnacle of success, and in so doing affirmed the validity and accessibility of the American dream. O. J. was proof that there were no class barriers in America, that someone could—even if they were born Black and poor— become an economic success in America by dint of their own talent and hard work. And, O. J. reassured white Americans that Black men, even big, strong, athletic black men, were no threat, were not dangerous, were even likable, and yes, good-looking. Smiling for the camera with his white (and blonde) wife, Nicole, and their beautiful children, O. J. seemed a testimonial to the promise of assimilation. This apparently had been so easily attainable for European immigrants and was, at long last, finally attainable for Black Americans. And then, with his arrest for the murder of his then ex-wife Nicole and her acquaintance Ron Goldman, this image transmogrified—at least for many white Americans—into the iconography of the brutal and dangerous Black man, driven to murder by his uncontrollable lust and jealousy for a white woman. The double-murder trial of O. J. Simpson is an important cultural marker for all that it says about Black masculinity.

Lee Atwater, Republican campaign adviser to George Bush in his successful race for President in 1988, proved just how effectively the cultural imagery of Black masculinity can be exploited for political gain. In the campaign Atwater vowed to make "Willie Horton—Dukakis' running mate" and proceeded to use the criminal record of one Black man, William Horton, to imply that Michael Dukakis was not "tough on crime." In the ads, reference was made to Dukakis's policy on prison furloughs and then to Horton's rape of a white woman while on one such furlough. On his death bed, Atwater apologized for his cynical and mean-spirited use of the Horton ads. But the apology came after the election was over, Atwater's candidate had prevailed, and the damage to American racial politics had been done.

The association between Black masculinity and criminality is a basic one in white supremacist ideology, whether extremist or not. And, the fact is that currently one out of four Black men is in the criminal justice system, whether in prison, on parole, or on probation, compared with only one in sixteen white men. This is used as *prima facie* evidence that Black men are inherently more violent and have a greater propensity for crime than white men. In reality, young Black and white men have similar rates of violence. These rates diverge only when white men begin to get older and get jobs; Black men do not get jobs and, as their rates of violence increase, have less likelihood of getting older,

White supremacist notions of the criminality of Black masculinity have very real consequences for the lives of masses of Black men. Black men are much more likely to become victims of police harassment and brutality; and Black men are much more likely to become victims of violence at the hands of other Black men. This is at least partially a symptom of internalized white supremacist notions of Black masculinity. Black women, too, suffer the consequences of white supremacist constructions of violent Black masculinity in the form of domestic violence at the hands of Black men, and a political system which is likely to see such behavior as what is expected rather than as a crime which should be punished.

Black Women

In 1991, Clarence Thomas sat before the House Judiciary Committee and referred to his sister as a "welfare queen" and as emblematic of what was wrong with contemporary domestic social policy. In 1992, candidate Bill

Clinton used a campaign speech to launch an attack against Sister Souljah, a young African American woman rapper, for her "racism" and used the opportunity to distance himself from Rev. Jesse Jackson and the core of Black voters he led. That two powerful men, one Black and one white, would single out relatively powerless Black women as sources of immense social problems is characteristic of white supremacist ideology.

White supremacist ideology takes a different shape as it is directed toward Black women. Although less visible than Black men in white supremacist discourse, Black women do exist within the text, often as the antithesis of white women. Indeed, Black women form a "key pillar" on which contemporary systems of domination rest (Collins, 1993:168). Collins outlines several images of Black women which provide "ideological justification for race, gender and class oppression" (Collins, 1990:70). Three of these images—mammies, matriarchs, and welfare mothers—involve constructions of Black motherhood. The image of the "mammy" is that of a Black mother, a "surrogate mother in blackface," caring for a white family. In the image of the asexual mammy, sexuality exists apart from fertility. In contrast to the "mammy," the "matriarch" is the image of a Black mother in a Black home. The "matriarch" is a bad mother, too aggressive for her or her family's own good, who fails to socialize her children properly. The third facet in this assemblage of controlling images of Black motherhood, and particularly relevant for this research, is the "welfare mother." The "welfare mother" represents a "failed mammy" who in contrast to the "matriarch" is not aggressive enough, is too accessible to her children, and is "content to sit around and collect welfare, shunning work and passing on her bad values to her offspring" (Collins, 1990:70–78).

Black Motherhood and "Welfare Queens"

When Black women do appear, as with white women, it is usually because of their reproductive abilities and their sexuality. Any similarities with the representations of white women end there, however. In stark contrast to the glorious portrait of motherhood for white women, motherhood for Black women is completely vilified.

The contrast between Black motherhood and white motherhood is at times explicitly drawn, as in a modified version of an illustration which appeared earlier (see figure IV.8). In the modified drawing, representations of women of other racial identities have been eliminated, and the two panels that remain depict a Black woman entering a "birth clinic" while a white woman enters an "abortion clinic" (*NAAWP*, no. 26, 1983, p. 7). The image

sets up a stark, dichoto-
mous relationship be-
tween the motherhood
of Black women and
that of white women,
in which Black women
are prodigious breed-
ers and white women
are reluctant partici-
pants in reproduction.

Black women are
frequently depicted
as mothers within
the publications, and
Black mothers are
portrayed as slothful,

Figure IV.8

drug-addicted, dishonest, and willful breeders of unwanted "non-white"
children. These themes converge in the common portrayal of the Black
woman as "welfare queen." "Welfare queens" are perpetrators of welfare fraud who live extravagantly and decadently on taxpayer's (read:
white men's) money while not working and blithely having additional
children to increase their welfare payments.

Two drawings, one from *WAR* and the other from *Racial Loyalty*, are
strikingly similar and illustrate this theme (see figures IV.9 and IV.10). In
the first image, a Black woman who is obviously pregnant smokes what appears to be a crackpipe, while taking various forms of aid from anonymous
white male hands (*WAR*, vol. 10, no. 1, 1991, p. 7). And in the second image, a Black woman receives her welfare check with a warning from the
white woman handing it to her to not "go spending it all on drugs" (*Racial
Loyalty*, no. 70, 1991, p. 12). Both drawings capture the most salient image
of Black women within this discourse, that of the "welfare queen."

The notion that Black women reproduce irresponsibly is a major com-
ponent of this image. An article published in *NAAWP* and written by an
unidentified white public school teacher highlights this theme. In the article, the teacher talks about one of her students, Danisha. Danisha is a
young Black girl whom the teacher suspects is pregnant. When the
teacher asks the student about her condition, this is what follows:

> Danisha immediately admitted that she was "with child," it was to be
> her second baby born before the end of her junior year. Why moth-
> erhood at such an early age? I asked. Whites tend to think in terms of
> being responsible and using common sense. She shocked me with

her reply, "You pays for 'em, I has 'em!" (*NAAWP*, no. 49, 1987, p. 3).

Figure IV.9

The author goes on to assert that Danisha's case is "not unique" for Black women, making the message here unmistakable. Danisha is "irresponsibly" with child, unlike whites who are responsible. And, supposedly by her own admission, Danisha is irresponsible enough not to care how she will take care of her baby because she knows that someone else "pays" while she "has 'em."

The "someone else" who pays for Danisha and the Black mothers she represents in white supremacist discourse is always the "white taxpayer." This message is repeated frequently and can be illustrated by an article and accompanying photograph found in the *Thunderbolt*. On the front page there is a photo of a Black woman and her eight children. The caption reads "Mary Odell and Her Welfare Family—You Are Paying for Their Breeding Millions!" (*Thunderbolt*, no. 255, 1980). The article never mentions the Black woman in the photo, but instead details the cost of welfare and welfare fraud. It then directly attributes the decline in money spent on military defense to these costs and predicts grievous consequences for the United States. The use of the photo with the text connects the ideas of welfare fraud to Black motherhood and places the burden for these directly on the white taxpayer.

Black women are also assumed to be living lives of leisurely hedonism as they receive government assistance. An example can be found in *NAAWP* in an article which appears with the headline, "Mother of 15 Loses Home in Spite of $42,500 a Year in Federal and Local Aid," alongside of which is a photo of an African American woman (*NAAWP*, no. 59, 1989, p. 7). The article and photo draw together the images of Black women who squander extravagant sums doled out by the government which they manage "irresponsibly."

While all of the publications share this image of Black women as "welfare queens," it is David Duke who has made this image a mainstay of the rhetoric of the *NAAWP* and used it as a cornerstone of his mainstream political career. According to Duke and the *NAAWP,* "America's True Enem[ies]," are the "capable but unwilling leeches" who are the primary recipients of welfare payments (*NAAWP,* no. 63, 1991, p. 4). Unmistakably, Black women are the "leeches" who are America's "true enemies."

The notion that Black women increase their number of children to increase their government assistance checks is pervasive. For instance, this point is made explicitly in "Welfare in America: Is It a Flop? Babies Entitle Negro Women to More Food Stamps and Other Welfare Benefits" (*NAAWP,* no. 32, 1984, p. 11). The article goes on to cite Charles Murray's

Figure IV.10

work in *Losing Ground* to support the argument that government aid programs have "destroyed individual initiative, undermined family life and created an army of people dependent on the dole" (p. 11). According to the article, the "most important" solution to the "welfare quagmire," is:

> trying some sort of birth control program for women who collect welfare. Women on welfare should not be allowed to have children . . . If [a woman on welfare] has another child anyway, she should be sterilized or lose her welfare payments. (*NAAWP,* special issue, 1984, p. 11)

Thus, it is Black women's fertility that is at the heart of the "welfare quagmire." The solution offered, the sterilization of Black women, leaves no doubt that government spending on welfare can be controlled if only Black women's fertility can be controlled. Duke goes on to blame a host of modern ills on Black women's fertility:

> We must stop paying black women to breed more low-I.Q. blacks who swarm in our major cities, turning them into one big slum full of crime, filth and disease. (*NAAWP*, special issue, 1984, p. 12)

In this passage, Duke not only lays the "welfare quagmire" at the feet of Black women, but he also attributes urban decay, crime, along with "filth and disease," to Black women's fertility.

Although there is a great deal of rhetorical energy expended in *NAAWP* and other publications about the wastefulness of welfare, all welfare recipients are not necessarily corrupt and undeserving. For instance, Duke comments that welfare is necessary in some cases, such as the following scenario:

> Now here's a person, he's out of a job, he's sick, he's hurt, he needs sustenance for himself and his family. (*NAAWP*, no. 37, 1986, p. 5)

However, the vast majority of welfare payments, according to white supremacists, do not go to such worthy (read: white, male) recipients, but rather to unworthy (read: Black, female) recipients, such as those featured in the illustrations.

Collins's explanation for the development of the image of the "welfare mother" is especially significant. She argues that this image is particularly effective in justifying race, gender, and class oppression. In terms of racial oppression, this image facilitates labeling African Americans as lazy for both the "welfare mother's" failure to work and her alleged failure to pass on the work ethic to her children. With regard to gender oppression, hegemonic constructions of gender and sexuality—in which women gain their primary identity, status, and sustenance from heterosexual marriage—are reinforced by vilifying "welfare mothers" as "unwed" and thus challenging a major tenet of male supremacy. Finally, in terms of class oppression, focusing attention on "welfare mothers" as the source of their own poverty precludes consideration of structural causes of economic inequality and thus strengthens established systems of inequality (Collins, 1990:77).

A fourth image of Black women which Collins explores is that of the "Jezebel," or the sexually aggressive/promiscuous woman. This image originated in the context of slavery as a way to justify the widespread sexual assaults on Black slave women by white men (Collins, 1990:77). In contemporary racist ideologies, this image is a particularly salient one because it connects Black women's sexuality to fertility and provides a rationale for the argument that minorities increase their population while whites commit "racial suicide" through low birthrates.

Black Women's Sexuality and the Case of Vanessa Williams

Black women's allegedly prolific fertility is attributed to an unrestrained sexuality which develops at an early age. For instance, in the article in *NAAWP* about "Danisha," the author relates a story about Danisha's sister, Yolanda. Yolanda is a high school senior who:

> spent a year with me in my consumer education class; my carefully planned lessons were no competition to the libidos she aroused with her tight, low-cut sweaters, a garment which allowed her to display an amazing crop of chest hair. Each day she would lean over my desk to ask a question, pointing her short-skirted backside toward the class causing slack jaws and eyes to bulge [*sic*]. (*NAAWP*, no. 49, 1987, p. 3)

In this passage, Yolanda is represented as sexually provocative, using her low-cut sweaters and short skirts to "arouse libidos" at every turn. This description of Yolanda is characteristic of those passages which refer to Black women's sexuality, which is repeatedly described as wanton and unrestricted.

Yet, while Black women are portrayed as promiscuous, they are also depicted as inherently unattractive. The reference in the previous quote to Yolanda's "large crop of chest hair," is indicative of this theme. Black women's lack of sexual attractiveness is perhaps best illustrated in an interview with David Duke first published in *Hustler* magazine, then reprinted in *NAAWP*.[6] In the interview, Duke is asked directly if he has ever slept with a Black woman. His response is telling:

> No! I just don't find them attractive. When I was visiting Southeast Asia, I didn't even sleep with a yellow woman. I just don't believe it would be right or moral. (*NAAWP*, no. 37, 1986, p. 5)

Here, Duke articulates one of the implicit messages about Black women within white supremacist discourse, that they are, by definition, unattractive, and hence, unappealing to white men.[7]

This theme of the unattractiveness of Black women is also evident in the illustrations of "welfare queens" featured earlier in this chapter. In these drawings, Black women are invariably featured as obese. Picturing them in this way constitutes them as asexual, in the context of a society in which to be thin and blonde (and white) is to be beautiful and sexually attractive.

In fact, Black women are seen as so unattractive that there are some instances in which they are likened to animals. For example, in an article from the *Torch* entitled, "Shocking Report (But Not Surprising)—Negress Mates with Baboon," the author goes on, tabloid-style, to recount the story of a Black woman who ". . . gave birth to a baboon baby" (*Torch*, no. 126, 1985, p. 4). The construction of Black women as animalistic confirms their status as unattractive and further distances their sexuality from white men.

Black women's sexuality represents a frightening potentiality to the framers of white supremacist discourse. In one illustration (figure IV.11) a svelte Black woman stands over a white man in dominatrix-fashion. The man wears a medallion which reads, "I'm a liberal." Behind the two figures are the letters "ERA" and the year 1989; and to the side is the caption, "What Chu Gonna Do *Now* White Boy?" (*WAR*, vol. 8, no. 3, 1989, p. 14). The woman in this drawing is not obese, and her stance and her attire suggest a sexuality at once untamed and controlling. The man in the drawing is only partially dressed and the garments he is wearing are suggestive of captive sexuality. The image intimates that if Black women were given power (presumably through the ERA) then white men would suffer sexually.

Given white supremacists' stance on

Figure IV.11

the inherent undesirability of Black women, Black beauty pageants are often the subject of ridicule in the publications.[8] Black women who participate in pageants are held up for derision and contempt because they are regarded as pretenders to a status, "beautiful," which they can never achieve. For instance, in the *Torch* a photo of an African American woman wearing a tiara appears under the caption, "What Is So Important About This Person?" The text answers:

> Actually there is *NOTHING* important about her. However, there is something interesting about her. She is one of 81 "Campus Queens at Black Colleges" listed in the April 1989 issue of *Ebony* magazine. (*Torch*, no. 134, 1989, p. 7)

There is no equivocation here in deciding that there "nothing" important about this woman. This quote is typical of the mockery reserved for Black women within white supremacist discourse. The remainder of the article goes on to address what is regarded as the bias inherent in Black beauty pageants.

Black beauty pageants are considered problematic because they are further evidence of rampant discrimination against whites. This is evident in the article just mentioned, in which the author deplores the "experience of having our pride verbally raped" by solicitations for the United Negro College Fund, while:

> to even suggest that Whites should be allowed to have a WHITE college or other institutions is sure to bring a barrage of slander and accusations denouncing our hate. (*Torch*, no. 134, 1989, p. 7)

Black institutions and organizations, whether beauty pageants or colleges, are represented as evidence of society-wide discrimination against whites. This theme is echoed in *NAAWP*. Beneath a photo of two African American women in evening gowns and tiaras, the headline "Miss Black New Orleans," appears and is followed by this text:

> The outcry that would result from a "Miss WHITE New Orleans . . . pageant is scarcely imaginable. Blacks demand both black-white integration and black-only segregation, but anything for whites only is impermissible. (*NAAWP*, no. 2, 1980, p. 5)

What this quote makes clear again is the perceived threat in Black-only organizations and institutions.[9] In both instances here, it is Black women in Black beauty pageants who are the embodiment of this menace.

All the more problematic within white supremacist discourse are pageants in which Black women compete directly with white women. One example appears in *Racial Loyalty*. A photo of an attractive, young African American woman appears under the banner, "The Problem . . ." and the caption reads:

> The above ugly mulatto nigger monkey has been nominated by the Jews as "Miss America" . . . White Man, how long are you going to tolerate such insults to the beauty of White woman by the perfidious, slimy Jews? (*Racial Loyalty*, no. 64, 1990, p. 11)

Below this is another which reads, "The Solution . . ." and there is a drawing of a white man in a cowboy hat, followed by the caption: "White Cowboy—The Symbol of White Manhood and Militancy."

Bracketing for now the references to Jews, the focus here is on the stark contrast set up here between "The Problem . . ." and "The Solution . . ." that highlights the images of Black women and white men established throughout the publications. Black women are "ugly" and "monkey[s]" while white men are the personification of "manhood" and "militancy" in the service of racial purity. Black women and white men are set against one another as opposites: Black women are clearly defined as "The Problem," while white men are the antidote.

The case of Vanessa Williams is particularly illustrative of the portrayal of Black women in white supremacist rhetoric. Vanessa Williams won the Miss America beauty pageant in 1984 and was the first African American woman ever to win the title. Just weeks before she was to complete her reign, sexually explicit photographs of Williams with a white woman were published in *Penthouse* magazine, and she was forced to resign. Several of the themes presented here concerning Black women converge in white supremacists' discussions of Williams's victory and the subsequent scandal.

Vanessa Williams's success in a pageant predominantly filled with white women is problematic in the context of a competition for which conformity to white standards of "beauty" is a prerequisite. For instance, the following excerpt from an article in *WAR* bemoans Williams's achievement:

> But what about the current labeling of Miss America? Miss America used to be the symbol of the exalted spiritual and sexual purity and chastity of the white woman, the envy of the world for her beauty . . . (*WAR*, vol. 4, no. 1, 1985, p. 4)

By being crowned "Miss America," Williams called into question white womanhood itself, with its attendant "exalted spiritual and sexual purity

103

and chastity." Williams's ascendance to the throne of Miss America challenges this as an exclusively white terrain and makes the value of white womanhood suspect.

There is a great deal of ambivalence around the subject of Williams's beauty. The dilemma raised by her victory surrounds the fact that Williams won a competition involving white women in which judges were asked to assess "beauty." The way this paradox is resolved is that Williams's beauty is never explicitly acknowledged, *and* it is simultaneously attributed to hypothetical white ancestors. For instance, in an article from the *Torch* called "A Black? Miss America," the author contends:

> while Vanessa Williams is hailed as the first black Miss America, she is actually anything but Negro. All the features that allowed her to win the title of Miss America were acquired from her white European ancestry. The features which are "typically black" . . . have been so watered down that they, if obvious, would surely have prevented her from gaining the title. (*Torch*, no. 123, 1984, p. 5)

This sentiment is repeated in the following excerpt from *WAR*:

> Big Brother still cannot push a midnight Black, half-ape, negro girl on White America and call her beautiful. The obvious disparity between the looks of the girl and the title of the pageant would be too great. So, instead, Big brother finds some semi-White woman who has three drops of negro blood from some distant grandparent. (*WAR*, vol. 4, no. 1, 1985, p. 4)

In both passages, Williams's beauty is implicitly acknowledged, yet explicitly denied as part of her "Blackness" and ascribed to her conjectural "white European ancestry." This attribution does not sanction Williams as white. Rather, despite these specific references to "white European ancestry," Williams remains firmly in the categorization "not white."

The scandalous photographs which prompted Williams's abdication of the Miss America title captured her engaged in cunnilingus with a white woman. Within white supremacist rhetoric, these photographs were corroborating evidence that Black women's sexuality is boundless and corrupt, as in this passage from *WAR*:

> She has since disgraced [the title] by acting like a typical negro of shoddy morals, by performing lesbian sex acts on camera . . . (*WAR*, vol. 4, no. 1, 1985, p. 4)

Williams's performance in the photographs is taken as confirmation of white supremacist claims of Black women's promiscuous, and here allegedly deviant, sexual nature. Williams's actions exemplify the "typical" and "shoddy morals" of Black women with regard to sexuality.

The saga of Vanessa Williams is a particularly illuminating example of the social and historical context of Black women's sexuality given the involvement of Tom Chiapel and Bob Guccione, two players in this drama who are barely mentioned in white supremacist accounts. The scandal unfolded when Tom Chiapel, a photographer for whom Williams had worked before entering the pageant, sold photos of her and another woman in sexually explicit poses to Bob Guccione, owner and publisher of *Penthouse*, a pornographic magazine. Guccione published the pictures, citing the public's "right to know." Williams denied that the photos reflected her own sexual practices, but rather were posed at the instigation of the photographer, Chiapel. Jackie Goldsby (1993) argues that the events surrounding Vanessa Williams's resignation had troubling similarities to the institution of slavery:

That Tom Chiapel presided over an auction at which he sold the photographs of Williams to the highest bidder; that Williams's body was sold to (re)produce higher profits for her "master," Bob Guccione . . . recalls the legacy of the sexual politics of American slavery. (Goldsby, 1993:122)

The former Miss America's protestations of "posing" rather than "spontaneously" engaging in the photos aside, Goldsby makes much of the fact that the photographs were of Vanessa Williams and another *woman*, rather than a man. She goes on to contend that by winning the Miss America pageant, Williams challenged:

the cultural maxim that Black women are objects of desire meant only for backroom trysts and not living-room-mantel material, and that the *Penthouse* photos publicized the continually denied fact that Black women do the nasty among ourselves and with female others. (Goldsby, 1993:124–25)

Indeed, Vanessa Williams's ascendance to the throne of Miss America contested racialized notions of femininity while her descent challenged notions of heterosexuality. As Collins writes, "Visible Black Lesbians challenge the mythical norm that the best people are white, male, rich, and heterosexual" (Collins, 1990:194). Although Williams denied (and continues to deny) she is a lesbian, her "performance" in the now infamous photographs visibly renders her a symbolic Black lesbian, and thus she subverts the mythical norm. It is precisely this potentially subversive quality of the photographs (and her ascendance to the throne, the *sine qua non* that give the photos their charged meaning) which situated Williams's within white supremacist discourse as the embodiment of Black women's "deviant" sexuality.

5

"ZOG," Bankers, and "Bull Dyke" Feminists: Jewish Men and Jewish Women

But the very concept of color is a quality of Otherness, not of reality. For not only are blacks black in this amorphous world of projection, so too are Jews.

—*Sander L. Gilman*, Difference and Pathology, *1985*

Jews exist in contemporary white supremacist publications within a complex and contradictory rhetorical space—definitely not white, yet deceptively so to extremists. The issue for white supremacists is not that Jews are "black," as Gilman suggests above, but rather that they are *not* white. Complicating matters are the dual realities that Jewish people in the context of institutionalized white supremacy in the United States are in the extraordinarily paradoxical position of identifying as "white" yet have a history and, for the most part, an ongoing consciousness of persecution and genocide rooted in their exclusion from the category "white." Further, American Jews are in the conflicted position of being "assimilated" in terms of economic, social, and political power while continuing to experience overt anti-Semitic attacks. Meanwhile, they simultaneously fear the loss of identity and the persecution associated with that identity. All in all, the prevailing social science literature seems to indicate that the contemporary United States is a good time and place to be a Jew (Dinnerstein, 1994; Lipset & Raab, 1995). Indeed, as one scholar notes, "much less prejudice exists in our own time than in any other period in the history of this nation" (Dinnerstein, 1994:243). Still, the fact remains that Jews are a primary target, indeed a central feature of, white supremacist discourse.

The historical persecution of Jews shows striking similarities with the modern racism directed at Blacks discussed previously. For centuries before the United States even existed, racist ideologies have regarded Jews as despicable creatures whose inferior physical, mental, and moral traits are inherited and passed on to successive generations, including a particularly unpleasant body odor. Jews were thought to suffer from diseases unknown to non-Jews, especially diseases of the blood. Such ideological constructions have been used to attribute a multitude of crimes to Jews, beginning with the murder of the pivotal figure of Christendom, Jesus, and including the murder of children for the purpose of using their blood in religious ritual. Central to the image of Jews in racist ideologies is the notion of a Jewish conspiracy, in which Jews are believed to manipulate much of the world's activities (Gossett, 1963:11; Mosse, 1978).

As in the centuries-old version, the notion of a Jewish conspiracy is central to contemporary white supremacist discourse. However, in the current rendering Jews are depicted as the behind-the-scenes manipulators of Blacks and whites on the stage of race relations. Even as viciously as Blacks are portrayed within white supremacist discourse, it is widely agreed that they are *not* the "real enemy" of the white race (e.g., *The Torch*, vol. 12, no. 9, pp. 6–7, "Jews are the Real Danger," and throughout). According to white supremacist discourse, Jews populate or control the United States government, "international banking and finance," and most industry. This power enables them to wield enormous influence over the course of world events. In white supremacist accounts, Jews were responsible for both the Lincoln and Kennedy assassinations, for the Vietnam and the Persian Gulf wars, as well as for the moral decay of American society at the end of the twentieth century. In a most sinister twist, their true power is seldom revealed because Jews also control our major source of information in this country, the news media (a.k.a., the "jewsmedia"). To further secure their hold over the American public, Jews have promoted television as *the* major recreational activity and filled it with propaganda and deception.

This is a broadly sketched version of the "Jewish conspiracy" as it is represented in white supremacist discourse. If we explore in detail what lies beyond this broad sketch we find a vision that is deeply embedded in notions of gender and sexuality. While much attention has been given to the construction of Black men as the dark Other, there has been relatively little scholarship on gendered images of Jewish men in racist ideologies (Brod, 1988 is an exception).

The Jewish conspiracy is a gendered notion. The individual Jews who are responsible for the conspiracy are gendered beings, and take on different and gendered tasks within the alleged cabal. To understand the Jewish conspiracy fully we must understand the representations of Jewish men and Jewish women within the publications.

Bankers and "ZOG"

The primary agent of the Jewish conspiracy is the Jewish man. As is clear from the illustration featured here, the embodiment of "The Evil Jew" is a Jewish man (see figure V.1) (*Racial Loyalty*, no. 70, 1991, p. 2). The two primary arenas in which Jewish men are believed to be at work in the Jewish conspiracy are the economy and government.

The most prevalent depiction of Jewish men within the publications is as bankers or financiers. Jewish men are believed to control both the United States and the international economies. Articles with titles such as "Jews Run Banks" (*Racial Loyalty*, no. 64, pp. 1–2 and throughout) are commonplace in the publications. It is Jewish *men*, specifically, who are portrayed as responsible for the control of banking and finance. For instance, in "Jewish Bankers Cause Economic Collapse and Unemployment," the accompanying illustration features only Jewish men (see figure V.2) (*Racial Loyalty*, no. 71, June 1991, p. 1). This is not a coincidence. In the white supremacist view, it is expressly Jewish men who are in positions of power in economic arenas. This control is not seen as a benign or benevolent despotism, however. Indeed, Jewish men in control of financial institutions are ruining the economy for everyone but themselves. In the article just men-

THE EVIL JEW

"WE WANT TO DESTROY THE WHITE RACE AND TAKE EVERYTHING YOU OWN."

Figure V.1

tioned from *Racial Loyalty*, Jewish men are portrayed as the source of unemployment and economic collapse (*Racial Loyalty*, no. 71, 1991, p. 1). An article in *The Klansman* portrayed the head of the Federal Reserve, Allan Greenspan, as a "master counterfeiter" based on his control of the monetary system (*The Klansman*, no. 148,

Figure V.2

1990, p. 11). And, white supremacists found it easy to incorporate the scandals on Wall Street during the 1980s into the discourse, as in the attempt at humor found in an article in *WAR* entitled "Would You Buy 2 Billion in Stock from This Man?" with an accompanying photo of Ivan Boesky (*WAR*, vol. 6, no. 1, 1987, p. 2).

Jewish men are also depicted as in control of the United States government, expressed by the acronym Z.O.G. (or J.O.G.). And, not surprisingly, it is white men who suffer most from this control, as in "Rev. Rudy Stanko is out of the clutches of the JOG's Gulags" (*Racial Loyalty*, no. 78, 1992, p. 1). Here, we see the theme of white men as patriots and martyrs repeated. This time, it is Rudy Stanko who is martyred because he is a prisoner of the Jewish Occupied Government.

Criminal Jewish Men

Much less prevalent than the representation of Jewish men as bankers or members of Z.O.G. is that of Jewish men as criminals. Rather than the omnipresent depiction of Black men as criminals, the representation of Jewish men in this way is relatively rare. Although the *Thunderbolt* features regular articles on the Leo Frank and Mary Phagan case,[1] appearances of this kind of story in the other publications is uncommon. However, those that do appear are worth considering.

In the instances in which Jewish men are featured as criminals they are, like Black men, represented as predatory murderers of white women. For example, in an article from *The Torch* under the headline, "Young Girl Brutally Murdered!," the publishers print a story about a young, white girl who is killed by a Jewish man (*The Torch*, vol. 9, no. 2, 1977, p. 1). And, in the article mentioned previously from *Racial Loyalty*, a Jewish man reportedly killed a white woman (*Racial Loyalty*, no. 60, 1990, p. 1). Although these instances are comparatively infrequent, they do fit the pattern established earlier of the representations of Black men as criminals. What seems to be different, however, is that Jewish men are more likely to be represented as "deceitful" or "treacherous" in the commission of their crimes, rather than "savage" or "animalistic" as are Black men.

Jewish Men as Threats to White Masculinity

Another popular theme within white supremacist discourse is Jewish men as threats to white masculinity. The rhetoric surrounding the threat to white masculinity is imbued with phallic and sexual imagery.

The perceived Jewish threat to white men's masculinity first appears in *Circumcision* infancy. Just as vasectomies are considered a form of sexual assault against white men, so too is circumcision. For example, this is discussed in "Circumcision: A Barbaric Jewish Ritual":

> Circumcision is being promoted primarily by the Jewish doctors because of their loyalty to the Jewish religious rituals. . . . Unfortunately, a great number of the White parents succumb to the Jewish propaganda and allow their newly born sons to be mutilated. (*Racial Loyalty*, no. 54, 1989, p. 8)

Here, white masculinity is represented as the penis-as-phallus, in the crudest biological sense, and it is this emblem of white masculinity which is portrayed as endangered by Jewish men and their scalpels.

The Jewish control of the economy is perceived as another threat to *economy* white masculinity. This threat is suggested in the following passage from *Racial Loyalty*:

> For generations, white middle-class men defined themselves by their careers, believing that loyalty to employers would be rewarded by job security and, therefore, the ability to provide for their families. But the past decade—marked by an epidemic of takeovers, mergers, downsizings and consolidations—has shattered that illusion. (*Racial Loyalty*, no. 66, 1990, p. 9)

Although this excerpt does not explicitly mention Jews, the intended message is difficult to miss as the article appears under the headline, "Jews Against White Men." The article intimates that Jewish men's control of the economy and the government are putting white men at a distinct disadvantage in achieving the traditional accoutrements of masculinity, chiefly economic success and the ability to "provide for their families."

This economic threat to white masculinity is graphically illustrated in this drawing published in *Racial Loyalty* (see figure V.3). Here, a white man is bent over kissing the shoe of a Jewish man. There is a sign that reads "U.S. Gov't" on a stick and the stick is inserted in the white man's buttocks (*Racial Loyalty*, no. 56, 1989, p. 12). Here, as in other images, masculinity is defined in relation to penetration: one who penetrates is masculine, one who is penetrated is not. The threat to white masculinity evident here is most immediately from the federal government, but it is a Jewish man who is in control of the scene, and it is he who represents the emasculating danger to white men.

The feminizing influence of Jewish men on white men, and the United States as a whole, is evident in the following illustration and accompanying article from *WAR* (see figure V.4). In the article, "North America's No. 1 Enemy," the author points out the dangers of Jewish control:

One of the characteristics of nations which are controlled by the Jews *is the*

YOU MISSED A SPOT ON
THE RIGHT SHOE, SLAVE.

Figure V.3

gradual eradication of masculine influence and power and the transfer of influence into feminine forms" [emphasis mine]. (*WAR,* vol. 8, no. 2, 1989, p. 14)

This quote indicates that Jewish men pose a threat to the masculinity of white men and the decline of all "masculine influence and power." What, exactly, it means to have power transferred "into feminine forms" is not clearly defined, but the implications of such a process for the United States are clear. The same article notes that Jews have "spawned a wave of homosexuality and degeneracy in America . . . (*WAR,* vol. 8, no. 2, 1989, p. 14). A decline in white masculinity apparently leads directly, irrevocably along one course, that is toward homosexuality and "degeneracy." The notion of degeneracy, equated with declining standards of culture, a devaluing of all that is accepted as "normal," good, and wholesome, and an attendant rise in disease, was also a key feature in Hitler's formation of the Third Reich. Much of his attacks against modern artists and the culture of the Weimar Republic were couched in very similar terms (Gilman, 1988). The degeneracy is very specifically linked to Jewish masculinity.

Jewish masculinity in the white suprema-

Figure V.4

cist imagination is threatening to white masculinity not because Jewish men are perceived as more "masculine," but because they are seen as effete, though not quite effeminate (or even homosexual), yet possessing the *sine qua non* of male dominance: economic power. This fact remains: Jews are depicted in a gender-specific way within the publications; and, specifically, "Jewish" means Jewish men. It is Jewish men who are the

113

bankers, the media moguls, the leaders of "Z.O.G." (and occasionally the criminals) that embody the white supremacist conspiratorial apparition.

Jewish Women

There has been relatively little scholarship on the images of Jewish women within racist ideologies. The work that does exist points to controlling images of Jewish women which, like those of both Black and white women, center around issues of sexuality and fertility. These themes take on a very different form when constructed about Jewish women. The sexuality of Jewish women is the focus of two common representations within popular culture: the Jewish Princess and the Jewish Mother. Jewish women as "JAPs," that is, "Jewish American Princesses," are spendthrifts who use sex to get material goods from rich husbands, but are otherwise withholding, especially sexually. In contrast, the "Jewish Mother" is a woman who is asexual, possibly sexually repressed and overinvolved in her family's lives (Beck, 1992). Ironically, these images do not appear that frequently within extremist white supremacist discourse. Within the context of extreme white supremacist discourse, Jewish women are discussed relatively infrequently compared to the volume of references to Jewish men as the embodiment of the evil Jewish Other. However, what discussion there is of Jewish women is illuminating.

Teachers, Not Mothers

In a striking divergence from the portrayals of either white women or Black women, and in contrast to the pervasiveness of the "Jewish mother" image in popular culture, Jewish mothers do not appear in the extremist white supremacist literature I studied. The social category of Jewish motherhood is completely effaced in extremist representations of Jewish women.

This is not to say that Jewish women are entirely absent from the publications. In fact, there is a connection between Jewish women and children, and it is established in their representations as teachers. As this illustration from *Racial Loyalty* demonstrates, Jewish women who are teachers are oppressing white children (see figure V.5). Here, a woman who appears to be a teacher, with a ruler at the ready, scowls while perusing an issue of *Racial Loyalty*. The caption above reads, "Miss

Goldberg's Class," and below, "Now I want to know, who brought this paper to class, that tells all these lies about us Jews? Don't you know you're guilty of anti-Semitism?" Here, the source of oppression for white children is "Miss Goldberg's" denial of the children's access to the "truth" as it appears in *Racial Loyalty.* Jewish women appear again as oppressive teachers in an article in *The Klansman.* In this text,

Figure V.5

a young girl is "prevented from giving out Christmas cards to her friends by a Jewish school teacher . . ." (*The Klansman*, no. 118–19, 1985, p. 7). As if this were not bad enough, insult is added to this perceived injury when the teacher:

> forced her second graders to watch her light Hanakah [*sic*] candles while she explained the illeged [*sic*] importance of this holiday to her captive audience. (*The Klansman*, no. 118-119, 1985, p. 7)

Here, the Jewish teacher is not only denying the children the exercise of their own, Christian religion, but also she is "forcing" her own Judaism on her "captive" second graders.

"Princesses"

A more common representation of Jewish women plays on the stereotype of the "Jewish Princess" or the "Jewish American Princess."

The depictions of Jewish women in white supremacist publications do not simply reproduce the stereotype of Jewish women as rich, pampered, and spoiled (Beck, 1990). Instead, white supremacist publications draw on the imagery of the "Jewish American Princess" to further mock Jewish women. Typically, the caricatures presented convey "mannish" or masculinized visions of Jewish women (see figure V.6). For instance, in *Racial Loyalty* a drawing of "The Classic Jewish Princess" appears in which a Jewish woman is unattractive, signaled by her large-sized, ill-fitting clothes, and "mannish," denoted by her hirsute legs, arms, and shoulders (*Racial Loyalty*, no. 62, 1990, p. 12).

A similar image takes the caricature a step further in case the reader missed the point (see figure V.7). In this illustration, below the Jewish "woman" appears the caption, "Hi!! I'm Miss Israel of 1989." This "woman" has breasts, and apparently, male genitalia, along with hairy arms, underarms, legs, and chest. The "mannish" view of

Figure V.6

Jewish women is here taken to a new extreme and the viewer is left to decide whether "Miss Israel" is man, a woman, or a "mannish" woman (*Racial Loyalty*, no. 46, 1989, p. 12). *NAAWP* repeats the same theme by drawing on images from the mainstream press. *NAAWP* uses a reprint of an editorial cartoon drawn by Oliphant, which includes a large woman dressed in fur coat and pearls with "Israel" written on her coat (*NAAWP*, no. 58, 1989, p. 12).

"Bull Dyke" Feminists: Threat to White Femininity

Certainly the most prevalent representation of Jewish women is as feminists and lesbians, two statuses that are often conflated with one another
in white supremacist discourse. This connection between Jewish women,
feminism, and lesbianism is seen as particularly threatening to white femininity.

In fact, the link between feminism and Jewish women is so fixed that
there is no mention of the women's movement that does not make reference to the Jewish leaders of the movement. One example of this connection can be seen in the following excerpt from *The Klansman*:

> It was the Jew who brought us Bella Abzug, Gloria Steinhem [*sic*],
> and the so-called "Women's Liberation Movement," with its atten-
> dant lesbianism.
> (*The Klansman*, no.
> 144, 1990, p. 4)

In this passage, the
connection between
Jewish women, such as
Bella Abzug and Glo-
ria Steinem, and femi-
nism, "the so-called
'Women's Liberation
Movement,'" and "its
attendant lesbianism,"
is set out with stark
clarity. Again, a photo
of Betty Friedan (with-
out an accompanying
article) appears with
this caption below the
photo:

> Jewess Betty Frie-
> dan, a founder of
> the anti-white femi-
> nist movement and
> current president
> of NOW (National

Figure V.7

117

Organization for Women), whose aim is to split Whites by gender. (*Racial Loyalty*, no. 71, 1991, p. 8)

Next to the photo is a final exhortation to white women who may have missed the point, "White Women, reject Jew-spawned suicidal feminism!"

The association between feminism and lesbianism can purportedly be traced to the historical roots of Judaism. In reference to the origins of the Star of David:

> The Talmud tells us that it comes from an inverse pubic triangle placed over an upright one. This blatantly lesbian symbol is perhaps the first sign of "Women's Lib." (*The Klansman*, no. 144, 1990, p. 4)

Here, one of the central icons of Judaism, the Star of David, is recast as a "blatantly" lesbian symbol, and is then read as an early sign of "Women's Lib." Again, in this recasting we see the link between feminism and lesbianism.

White women who advocate a semblance of equality in the white supremacist movement are distinguished from the Jewish women of the "Jew dyke conspiracy," that is, feminists. This distinction was made clear in an article that appeared just two issues after the first mention of the Aryan Women's League (AWL) and the accompanying illustration of white women as "racial warriors" (see chapter 3). This article was written by a white man identified as "Baxter the Pagan" and as the husband of the woman who started the AWL. The article is entitled, "From a Man's Point of View," and it addresses the problem that the AWL has created for some men in the movement. Indeed, the author confesses:

> When she started the Aryan Women's League, I questioned how far it would go, and if it would be some new wave of feminist E.R.A. crap that would antagonize an already divided movement. (*WAR*, vol. 8, no. 4, 1989, p. 14)

His fears were allayed and he became a supporter of the AWL because "The AWL isn't some Jew-dyke-we-hate-White-males type of deal" (*WAR*, vol. 8, no. 4, 1989, p. 14). He goes on to explain what "type of deal" the AWL truly is:

> Our women wage major campaigns against the anti-White women as a whole and especially the Jew/dyke dictatorship that controls the women's action groups. These khazar lesbos turn packs of zombie

women into dykes in matters of hours, in mass public rallies and demonstrations! (*WAR*, vol. 8, no. 4, 1989, p. 14)

The crucial distinction being made here is between white women who want to make claims of equal status with white men as racial warriors, and Jewish women who are seen as part of the "Jew-dyke-conspiracy" to divide the white race.

The image of the "Jew dyke" is a relatively rare one in white supremacist publications, but it does appear once in an issue of *WAR* (see Figure V.8). The illustration featured here is of Jewish "bull dyke," identifiable as Jewish by the prominent nose, and as a lesbian by the symbol tattooed on her arm. The woman is the central figure in this drawing. The background of the picture is a street scene filled with signs of the decay and degeneracy of contemporary, racially-mixed society: two gay men kissing, a homeless man, two obese Black women in various stages of undress, advertisements along the street for an "AIDS Clinic," "Ginzburg Bail Bonds," "Interracial Enema Videos," and "Beer-N-Wine." At the center of this debauchery is the Jewish "bull dyke" accosting a young, white boy (the only white in the drawing). The caption beneath the drawing reads,

> I saw you throw that candy wrapper on the ground. It's dirty little goy boys like you who are making this world so ugly. (*WAR*, vol. 8, no. 3, 1989, p. 4)

Figure V.8

In this symbolically rich illustration, we see several themes concerning Jewish women repeated. First, the woman drawn here signifies, with her shaved head, tattooed arm, large frame, and ill-fitting clothes, the "mannish" and unattractive attributes consistent with the earlier discussion of Jewish women. And second, we see a connection being made between Jewish women and white children, a connection that is represented as inherently oppressive to white children. Here, despite all the supposed "depravity" going on around the Jewish woman, it is the white boy that she singles out for her scolding attention. The representation of lesbians as mannish, or masculine, is rhetorical strategy which works in contradictory ways. On the one hand, it is intended as an insult, and as such is an effective mechanism of social control; yet, on the other hand, it encapsulates the instability of gender, calling into question categories of male/female and masculine/feminine (Roof, 1993).

Consequences of the "Jew dyke conspiracy" are potentially catastrophic for white femininity. Jewish women are perceived to be threats to white reproductivity, the white family, and specifically, to the sexuality of young white women.

The reproduction of the white race depends on the reproductive complicity of white women, as discussed previously (see chapter 3). This complicity is threatened by the "so-called 'Women's Liberation Movement' and its attendant lesbianism," mentioned in the quote above. The passage goes on to spell out the implications of the "Women's Liberation Movement" for the white race:

> Our [white] women were liberated alright; they were taken from their husbands, families and home and were put to work for the Jews. *This more than any other thing is responsible for the zero population growth of the white race* [emphasis mine]. (*The Klansman,* no. 144, 1990, p. 4)

Here, feminism is responsible, "more than any other thing," for the declining fertility of the white race. Clearly, it is Jews, and specifically Jewish women, who are held to be most culpable for this decline.

Along with the threat to white reproductivity, Jewish women are a threat to the white family. In an article in *Racial Loyalty* entitled "Stop the Jew Induced Decline of the White Family," among the list of proscriptions is this:

> We must reject the Jew-propagated feminism ("ERA," "women's lib," "sexual revolution," and all the other accompanying nonsense) as an artificial, false concept, which is harmful to both White women and White men. By promoting feminism among White women, Jews aim to divide the White Race and sabotage the natural cycle of procreation [emphasis in the original]. (*Racial Loyalty,* no. 53, 1989, p. 9)

In this quote, we see that "Jew-propagated feminism" and "all the other ac-companying nonsense" is again implicated in the deterioration of the white family by dividing white women and white men and sabotaging "the natural cycle of procreation." Although this passage does not specifically refer to Jewish women, the connection established between "Jew-propa-gated feminism" and Jewish women is so well-defined that the mention of Jewish women here would be redundant.

Yet another threat to white femininity from Jewish women is related to the sexuality of young, white women. While the sexual threat of Jewish women is not a prevalent theme in the publications, its appearance is sig-nificant. This threat surfaces in an article mentioned previously, entitled "It's the Law," which speculates about what the future will hold when "Z.O.G." takes over. To reiterate, the passage is as follows:

> When it becomes the law of the land that every white man with a daughter between 12 and 17 years of age, must bring her to an inter-racial bi-sexual sensitivity class he will obey, for it is the law. There his daughter will alternately be raped and sodomized by Negroes and bull dyke Jewesses. (*WAR*, vol. 4, no. 3, 1985, p. 10)

Here, the threat to young, white women is perceived to be from "Ne-groes," presumably men. This is not surprising given the dual representa-tions of white women as victims and targets of sexual assault and of Black men as rapists of white women. What is striking is that "bull dyke Jewesses" are seen as just as threatening to the sexuality of young, white women as Black men. This characterization of Jewish women as "bull dykes" is com-mon throughout the publications; what is less frequent is the element of sexual threat implied in this quote.

Jewish men and Jewish women play very different roles in the Jewish conspiracy, according to white supremacist discourse. Jewish men control government, the economy, and the media; Jewish women attempt to di-vide the white race by gender through the use of feminism. Given the gen-dered nature of the alleged conspiracy, what remains then is to examine what the ulimate goal of this conspiracy is and how it is to be accom-plished within white supremacist discourse.

"Race-Mixing": White Supremacist Dystopia

White supremacist themes and images about Jewish men and Jewish women, Black men and Black women, and white men and white women converge in discourse concerning "race-mixing." This occurs simultane-

121

segregated housing)

ously on two levels, the group and the individual. White supremacists advocate the complete separation of people based on racial categorization. One aspect of this theme is the advocacy of racially segregated housing. The message that whites should live only with whites is underscored in articles recounting the horrendous consequences faced by those who choose not to live in racially segregated areas. For example, a series of articles in *Thunderbolt* appeared under the banner, "Move Into Black Areas Means DEATH!" (*Thunderbolt*, no. 252, 1980, p. 5). One article tells the story of a white woman who "was a cultured lady but unfortunately a liberal thoroughly indoctrinated with the dangerous philosophy of racial equality" (*Thunderbolt*, no. 252, April 1980, p. 5). The article goes on to describe the "fiendish torture" of the woman; and, although there is no mention of who is responsible for the woman's death, the implication is clear as the article concludes that the neighborhood has continued to "deteriorate back to the ways of the Darkest Jungles of Africa." As if the moral of this story is not plain enough, it is crystallized for the reader; "Her lifetime devotion to the cause of race-mixing had come to a gruesome and grisly end" (*Thunderbolt*, no. 252, 1980, p. 5).

The inevitable outcome of "race-mixing" at the group level is "race-mixing" at the individual level. In "Taxes Used to Move Blacks," the ultimate goal of integrated housing is explicated:

> On this page we show a shocking photo of a negro in the suburbs riding with a group of his White friends. It will not be long before he asks one of their sisters for a date. She will agree so as not to break up her brother's friendship. As young Whites and blacks grow up together and socialize as friends, there can be no doubt that interracial marriage and mongrelization of the races will increase at a rapid pace. (*Thunderbolt*, no. 232, 1978, p. 5)

The racial integration of housing provides a context in which themes of Black men as sexually aggressive and white women as potential racial traitors because of their sexuality join. This convergence is said to lead inexorably to interracial marriage and the "mongrelization" of the races. The relationships set forth in this quote also illustrate the most prevalent portrayal of "race-mixing" in white supremacist discourse.

The standard representation of "race-mixing" is one in which *Black men and white women* are the principal actors. Indeed, this is arguably the central metaphor within this discourse. Every publication, and virtually every issue, contains some reference to this particular configuration of "race-mixing." An example of one of these references appears in an article from

NAAWP titled "Racial Integrity!" It is a call for racial "purity," and it begins by referring to ideas of racial integration:

> The theory . . . was that once the different races are broken down we can enjoy a world of peace, love, harmony and plenty! The elimination of race and racial differences would mean the end of hatred, greed and envy! . . . Interracial dating and marriage was presented as a way to usher in that brave new world. (*NAAWP*, no. 38, 1986, p. 1)

The article reiterates the theme that "race-mixing" on a group level leads inevitably to "race-mixing" on an individual level. Also included is a photo which leaves no doubt about the precise version of "race-mixing" being addressed. The photo is one of a Black man and a white woman kissing, and the caption reads, "Race-mixing: Symbol of Decadence in a Once Proud People." Obviously, it is Black men with white women who are the embodiment of the threat of "race-mixing."

Figure V.9

An article from *Racial Loyalty* highlights this theme as well. "Racial Hygiene: Eugenics vs. Mongrelization raises concerns about the

> poisoning [of the] White gene pool, pulling the White Race down slowly but surely, until we will be a miserable and shameful mass of idiotic brown zombies, docile, stupid and ready to be willing slaves. (*Racial Loyalty*, no. 62, 1990, pp. 1–3)

Accompanying this text is a photo of a Black man and a white woman with the caption, "The White Beauty and the Nigger Beast! *The Worst Crime*

Against Race and Nature!" [emphasis in the original]. Again, it is Black men with white women who are the symbol of "race-mixing."

A cartoon, which appeared in the *Torch*, further illustrates this theme (see figure V.9). The protagonist in the cartoon is a white man who is putting up leaflets that read, "White People Fight! For the Future of your Children SMASH RACE-MIXING," when he encounters a Black man and a white woman in an alley coming out of what appears to be a bar. The white man sprays them with tear gas and attacks them both, leaving the Black man on the ground and the white woman in a trash can. In the last panel of the cartoon, the white man returns to his home and realizes that his act "may not have furthered the revolution, but it satisfied the soul!" (*Torch*, vol. 12, no. 9, 1981, p. 11). In this example of the "race-mixing" theme, it is again Black men and white women who are perpetrators of this "racial crime." Further, it is white men who are depicted as racial patriots, defending "racial integrity" against this crime.

There are exceptions to this pattern, but mentions of *white men and black women* are extremely rare. Often allusions to this type of "race-mixing" reference different historical eras, placing such occurrences in the distant past. These discussions also lack the virulence of those that concern black men and white women. One mention occurs in *Racial Loyalty* in which the author writes of the conquest of Santo Domingo, "The scarcity of White women had made illicit relations between white colonists and female blacks inevitable from the first" (*Racial Loyalty*, no. 8, 1984, p. 6). The use of the term "inevitable" to describe this sexual contact between white men and black women is striking when contrasted with the rhetoric reserved for those white women and black men who would dare to cross such boundaries. Still, the exceptions serve to highlight the emphasis placed on the type of "race-mixing" which is deemed most perilous, that which occurs between Black men and white women.

What is significant in the trope of the Black man and white woman is that Black women are missing from this central metaphor. Their exclusion is not an inadvertent oversight but an expected, even inevitable, outcome based on a tension created through a series of dichotomous relationships established within the discourse. The first and most obvious tension is that between "Blackness" and "whiteness." They are characterized as oppositional entities: one the incarnation of evil, the other the manifestation of truth, beauty, and purity. To mix these two essences would be to dilute and ultimately lose what remains in the world of "goodness."

The second dichotomy is between Black women and white women. Black women are depicted as unattractive; white women are the embodiment of beauty. White women, because they are so beautiful, are highly prized by Black men, according to white supremacist discourse. Indeed, white women's beauty inspires an insatiable sexual lust in Black men. Yet, despite their depiction as innately promiscuous, Black women arouse no such longing in white men. In fact, Black women are portrayed as so utterly undesirable, especially to white men, as to be inhuman. Thus, Black women are eliminated from the pivotal drama of "race-mixing" because of their construction as unattractive.

Third, Black women are absent from this central metaphor because white men are racial patriots; but white women are potentially racial traitors. Since "race-mixing" is tantamount to racial treason, white men, given their representations as racial warriors, martyrs, and heroes, are presumed to be above such sexual betrayals to their racial identity. White women, however, are not immune to such sexually inspired racial disloyalty.

Black men, rather than being subsumed within the category of "Black," are singled out as unique targets of white supremacist discourse. Black men are almost universally represented as criminals, as economic and political threats and incompetents, and they are viewed as sexual threats to both white women and white men. The one apparent exception to this representation, the story on James Meredith, is only a thinly veiled attempt to convey the message that Black men pose a serious political threat to white hegemony.

Black women, like white women, are portrayed in ways which emphasize their sexuality and reproductive abilities; yet, at the same time, Black women are depicted as the very antithesis of white women. Black women are most frequently represented as "welfare queens." Black women's sexuality is particularly problematic in the discourse, as they are rendered at once unattractive and promiscuous; at once sexually unappealing and yet threatening to white men. The discussion of the former Miss America, Vanessa Williams, and the scandal surrounding her reign highlights many of these themes.

Images of Black men, Black women, white men, and white women converge in white supremacist rhetoric concerning "race-mixing," which is the central metaphor in the discourse.

The rearticulation of "whiteness" is predicated on the constitution of "Blackness," which inheres in this series of dichotomies. Within the discourse, notions of "whiteness" rely upon those of "Blackness" for meaning, and each of these racial categorizations, in turn, depend on hegemonic constructions of gender and sexuality.

Jews and Race-Mixing, Abortion, and Homosexuality

In an amazing and profound reversal of historical reality, the goal of the alleged Jewish conspiracy is the genocide of the white race. There are, according to white supremacists, three main strategies involved in this conspiracy: "race-mixing," abortion, and homosexuality. These strategies are as interwoven with issues of gender and sexuality as are the conspirators.

The preeminent Jewish tactic for eliminating the white race is "race-mixing" or the "mongrelization" of the white race through interracial marriage, and the resulting interracial offspring. One publication referred to the "mongrelization of the white race" as the "ultimate horror and the worst crime against nature" (*Racial Loyalty*, no. 72, 1991, p. 3).

race-mixing

There is no mistaking who is behind this "ultimate horror"; it is the Jews. For instance, in the illustration here (see figure V.10), a white woman brings a Black man home to meet her parents and says, "Mom . . . Dad, I'd like you to meet Leroy, my new boyfriend." The caption reads, "What the Jews Are Trying to Accomplish!" (*Racial Loyalty*, no. 62, 1990, p. 12). The match between the young woman in the illustration and "Leroy" is the "ultimate horror" for white supremacists. They argue that the Jewish-controlled media fosters a climate in which "race-mixing" is acceptable. The only mention that cultural icon Madonna receives in these publications is in an article concerning her appearance with a Black man in a soft drink advertisement. The ad is presumably a creation of the Jewish men who con-

Figure V.10

trol the media, and the author states in no uncertain terms: "What these bastards are selling is the destruction of our people through race-mixing with Congoids" (*Racial Loyalty*, no. 50, 1989, p. 12).

The Jewish-controlled media works in other ways to promote "race-mixing" and the eradication of the white race. In "Genocide through Race-Mixing: Jewish Plot Against the White Race," Eric Thomson writes:

> Some investigators feel that this genocidal behavior is rooted in the work of the Jewish media-dominators who have made massive propaganda to feminize White males and to masculinize White females over the decades. (*Racial Loyalty*, no. 72, 1991, p. 3)

In this quote, the Jewish men who are the "media-dominators" are at work trying to "feminize White males" and "masculinize White females."

This is a contributing factor to the pervasive problem of "race-mixing" primarily for white men. Elsewhere in this same article, in one of the very few instances acknowledging that white men may engage in "race-mixing," Thomson writes:

> In this era of Jew-spawned feminism, how often does one hear the complaint that White women are too demanding and too difficult to live with? Many White males who feel this way . . . seek out colored females whom they consider "more feminine," that is, more submissive and attentive to male needs than the White female. (*Racial Loyalty*, no. 72, 1991, p. 3)

Clearly, if white men are engaging in the "worst crime" of "race-mixing" it is because white women, inspired by "Jew-spawned feminism," have driven them to it by being "too demanding and too difficult to live with." There is no analogous reasoning in this article, or anywhere else in the publications, for white women who are compelled to seek out Black or Jewish men. White women here are more culpable than white men, but it is Jewish women who are the most responsible because of their connection to feminism.

Jewish men, too, are implicated in the temptation of white men into the crime of "race-mixing," as in the illustration featured here (see figure V.11). The caption to this image reads, "The Jews Want to Mongrelize the White Race." In the drawing, it is a Jewish man who is whispering to a white man, "Psst . . . Have you ever thought of marrying a nice black woman? Look at all the half-breeds you could produce" (*Racial Loyalty*, no. 62, 1990, p. 1). This illustration is noteworthy because it is one of the very few instances in which even the possibility that white men could participate in "race-mixing" is entertained. And, it is important because it epitomizes the white supremacist view of the role Jewish men play in promoting "race-mixing" among white men.

Yet, for all the animosity toward Jews, both men and women inherent in these images, there remains a certain ambivalence about, even grudging respect for, the Jews around the issue of "race-mixing." For instance, in the article mentioned previously, "Stop the Jew Induced Decline of the White Family," there is a passage concerning what to do if the daughter of a racially loyal white family decides "without any regard for the

Figure V.11

interests of their family and even their race," to choose "Jews, muds, or even niggers as [her] reproductive partner . . ." (*Racial Loyalty*, no. 53, 1989, p. 9). The only correct response in such a case, according to the author, is:

> the one practiced by the racially loyal Jews. They excommunicate, disinherit their family traitors, and conduct a symbolic funeral ceremony, because a child who betrays his family and his race is already racially dead. (*Racial Loyalty*, no. 53, 1989, p. 9)

In this passage we see a very different portrayal of Jews. Here, it is Jews who are the ones to emulate when it comes to dealing with issues of "race-mixing" and racial traitors (note that again it is a white woman who is featured in this allegory as the racial traitor, as discussed in chapter 3), even though they are so thoroughly implicated in this strategy to eradicate the white race.

128

Jews and Abortion

As previous discussions indicated, abortion is racialized within white supremacist discourse, so that white women who have abortions are depicted as racial traitors and Black women who do not have them are enemies of the white race. And, abortion is also seen as a another Jewish tactic to destroy the white race. One of the major points of evidence white supremacists use to support the notion of abortion as a Jewish conspiracy is the contention that most of the doctors who perform abortions are Jewish. For example, in "White Genocide," the author points out ". . . the majority of doctors in urban areas giving abortions are Jewish" (*WAR*, vol. 3, no. 5, 1984, p. 2). There seems to be wide agreement within the discourse that those performing abortions are Jewish. However, there are differing ideas about whether these doctors are Jewish men or Jewish women.

In one illustration from *Racial Loyalty*, several themes come together (see figure V.12). In the image, a white man is tied down over a map of the United States. To the side are two Jewish men, and one is saying to the other, "Gee, Rabbi Finklestein, I hope he doesn't realize we Jews ripped him off and aborted his family" (*Racial Loyalty*, no. 53, 1989, p. 13). Here, the overriding theme is one of Jewish men in control of white men. This is exhibited through Jewish control of banking, finance, and economics: "we Jews ripped him off." And, it is Jewish men who are the culprits in the racial crime of abortion, for it is they who have "aborted his family."

Figure V.12

However, it is not Jewish men who are universally represented as responsible for white abortions. In fact, it is more commonly Jewish women who are portrayed as the culprits. In another image, a white woman warns other white women of the racial aspect of abortions and those who perform abortions (see figure V.13). The full text of the warning is:

Did you know that most abortionists are Jewish or other non-whites
. . . and that the pro-abortion movement is headed by unfeminine
feminist Jewesses who counsel non-whites to not get abortions . . .
and did you know that abortionists slaughter nearly one million
white babies every year? Jewish ritual murder is alive and well in the United States of America . . . and is very legal! (*WAR,* vol. 8, no. 3, 1989, p. 4).

Figure V.13

Again, we see the theme of Jewish women as "unfeminine" repeated, and it is these "unfeminine feminist Jewesses" who are behind the "pro-abortion movement" and "Jewish ritual murder." Thus, whether it is Jewish men or Jewish women who are the primary actors, it is Jews who are the foremost proponents of abortions for white women, in the interest of the genocide of the white race.

Jews and Homosexuals

Jews and homosexuals, like feminists and lesbians, are two groups within the discourse which are often conflated with one another. Homosexuals, whether gay men or lesbians, who are Jewish are especially spotlighted; Jews who are not homosexual are depicted as promoters and advocates of homosexuality. For example, the *Torch* refers in several places to the late

San Francisco supervisor, Harvey Milk, as a "Jew Queer Activist" (*The Torch*, no. 120, 1984, p. 14 and throughout).

Jewish support for particular political candidates is pointed to as evidence of an affinity for homosexuals. In an article concerning the Massachusetts Representative entitled, "Even Though He Is a Queer . . . Jews Still Love Barney Frank!" the focus of the article is both on Frank's homosexuality and his Jewish identity (*The Torch*, no. 138, 1991, p. 4).

Given white supremacist assumptions about Jews' power in society and their love for homosexuals, they draw the logical—and frightening—conclusion that Jews are trying to force homosexuality and gay rights laws onto unwilling citizens. An article with the provocative title, "Christian School Forced to Hire Homosexual Teacher!" appears in *The Torch*, and the first line of the article reads, "The above headline has not occurred—yet. But if presidential hopeful Walter Mondale and the perverts have their way it soon will" (*The Torch*, no. 114, 1982, p. 1). The author goes on to offer a dystopian vision of what would happen with the advent of gay rights laws:

> You could not hire help or rent an apartment without the intrusion of this law. And the evil little kike jew lawyers who dominate the NAACP, ACLU, Southern Poverty Law Center, etc., would be paid in *your tax* dollars to ensure this vile, filthy law was enforced in every area of your life [emphasis in the original]. (*The Torch*, no. 114, 1982, p. 6)

Here, it is Jewish lawyers who will carry out the marching orders of a gay rights law (mandated no doubt by Z.O.G.) and demand compliance from recalcitrant, heterosexual taxpayers. Within white supremacist discourse, homosexuality and Jewishness are intertwined in a most complex manner.

This connection is also clear in more mainstream discussions of Jews and homosexuality, both historically and in the contemporary context. Throughout much of European history, the fate of gay people and Jews has been continually linked by opposition from Christendom and the Third Reich. As historian John Boswell has noted:

> The same laws which oppressed Jews oppressed gay people; the same groups bent on eliminating Jews tried to wipe out homosexuality; the same periods of European history which could not make room for Jewish distinctiveness reacted violently against sexual nonconformity; the same countries which insisted on religious uniformity imposed majority standards of sexual conduct; and even the same methods of propaganda were used against Jews and gay peo-

131

ple—picturing them as animals bent on the destruction of the children of the majority. (1980:15–16)

Boswell links the contemporary intolerance toward gays and lesbians not to Christianity (indeed, he provides convincing evidence of the tolerance among early Christians for same-sex unions) but rather to the development of capitalism. According to Boswell, the "transition from tolerance to hostility . . . was almost wholly the consequence of the rise of corporate states and institutions with the power and desire to regulate increasingly personal aspects of human life" (1980:37).

Summary

Anti-Semitism is in many ways the historical antedecent to both contemporary racism directed toward Blacks and homophobia. There is an ongoing debate within the social science literature about the level and relative significance of anti-Semitism in the United States today. I want to suggest that to the extent that Jews may appropriate "whiteness," that is, see themselves and have others view them as "white," anti-Semitism decreases and is generally less threatening. However, when Jews become racialized, that is, when they move away from or out of the racially unmarked category that is "whiteness" (those who occupy the social category of "white ethnic" are seen as capable of appropriating) into the space of racial Other, they become targets of anti-Semitism and the same discourse that targets Blacks. Jews have been successful within a white supremacist context to the extent to which they have been able to appropriate whiteness. Within this extremist literature, Jews are most certainly not seen as white; they are designated as racial Others, but this designation is not without ambiguity.

The perceived danger posed by Jews within the discourse is that they, like gays and lesbians, are seen as a threat from within because they can each "pass" effectively in ways that are not possible for most Blacks in this society.

Ironically, the contemporary lesbian and gay movement in the United States has adopted a rhetoric which posits an analogous position and treatment to Blacks before the civil rights movement, a strategy which presumes an alliance where there is often none, and which alienates many African Americans who find such an analogy offensive. I say ironically because the stronger association and better link is to the treatment of Jews. There is much historical precedent for this link, including the shared history of persecution of Jews and lesbians and gays in Nazi Germany.

6

The Ends of White Supremacy

*These white folk have newspapers, magazines, radios, spokesmen to get
their ideas across. If they want to tell the world a lie, they can tell it so
well that it becomes the truth; and if I tell them that you are lying, they
will tell the world even if you prove you're telling the truth. Because it's
the kind of lie they want to hear . . . .*

—*Dr. Bledsoe to the hero in Ralph Ellison's* Invisible Man

The lie that white folk have told (and believed) over and over again is that
"race" is an effective marker of intellectual and moral superiority and inferiority. It is a lie that is predicated on another lie: that "race" is an inherently meaningful, indeed naturally occurring, category. It is clear,
however, that even in the most extremist literature the supposedly im-
mutable classification of "race" requires a great deal of rhetorical construction to be sustained. White supremacist discourse is preoccupied
with efforts to overcome the ambiguities and shore up the inconsistencies
of racial categorization by setting out precisely who is—and is *not*—
"white," "Black," and "Jewish." These categories, mutually exclusive and
ontologically exhaustive, are the foundation on which the rest of white supremacist logic (if it can be called that) is built.

"Race" is inextricably connected to notions of gender and sexuality.
Thus, while it may be that reference is made to "whites" as a racial group,
what it means to be a "white man" is qualitatively different from what it
means to be a "white woman." What this means in terms of our theoretical understanding of the connections between race, class, gender, and

133

sexuality is that although it may be possible to separate out race from class, or from gender, or from sexuality *heuristically*, it is not possible to do so in any way but the most conceptual. Black feminist scholars have demonstrated this in terms of the impossibility of delimiting race from class from gender in the realm of lived experience (see, for example, Collins, 1991). I have attempted to demonstrate here that this inseparability is also true for those who actively imagine and work to sustain white supremacy in its most extreme and offensive expressions. I contend that the very process of creating white supremacist discourse (and white supremacy more broadly) is inextricably linked with the formation of class, gender, and sexuality as categories of oppression.

My argument here has been that understanding white supremacist discourse depends on our ability to set aside our revulsion at these images for a moment and begin to take the message they offer seriously. In this discourse, race, class, gender, and sexuality are inscribed on bodies that are racialized/sexualized as Others. These bodies are stand-ins for larger racialized categories—white, Blacks, Jews—and their place in the white supremacist imagination. Not coincidentally, these categories most often take on corporeality in the racialized and sexualized bodies of men.

White supremacist ideology is, as Cornel West (1993) has noted, first and foremost about the degradation of Black bodies in order to control them; it is also about the degradation of Jewish bodies and gay bodies. And, frequently (though by no means exclusively), it is about the degradation of certain men's bodies through the dominance of other men's bodies.

The domination portrayed here is not disconnected from broader society. This discourse utilizes extreme images that both create racism and reflect core, mainstream values of the United States. Surely part of the explanation for why white supremacist ideologies remain intractable features of the political landscape (Bell, 1992; Goldberg, 1993) lies in the way white supremacy hinges on class antagonism as well as notions of gender and sexuality for its justification. The challenges of the 1960s and 1970s from a variety of political movements effectively called into question not only "whiteness" (Omi & Winant, 1986), but also "white masculinity" and the normative constraints implicit in a white, male, heterosexual center. While such challenges have succeeded in making explicitly racist claims socially unacceptable, this change signifies that such sentiments have merely been subordinated (and sublimated?), rather than eliminated, and given voice only in a cultural and ideological space designated as "extremist."

I am not arguing that white supremacist discourse is not extreme, it most certainly is. Rather, I contend that the widespread appearance of

134

many white supremacist motifs in popular culture, with many of the connections between race, class, gender, and sexuality laid out here still intact, suggests that such themes resonate effectively beyond the audience of avowed white supremacists. Indeed, to recall just one example, the use of the Willie Horton advertisement in the 1988 Bush campaign (or any random sample of network news broadcasts on the topic of "crime") attests that the black-man-as-beast imagery of the white supremacist drawing, "Today's Young Coon," is not far removed from mainstream politics. Just as the degrading images of women in some heterosexual pornography are rejected for pushing the bounds of excess, strikingly similar images of women are embraced when they appear in mainstream advertisements for perfume, underwear, or bathing-suit editions of men's magazines. The point remains, however, that despite the extreme, often crude nature of white supremacist rhetoric, this work demonstrates that the discourse if taken seriously can provide us with important insights.

The fact that this discourse shares much in common with mainstream political discourse and popular culture representations has serious political implications. For instance, the rise of the Third Reich was built on just such imagery. In the current era, when "ethnic cleansing" has once again become a feature of the political landscape in Europe, it is vital that we contemplate the implications for the United States. To take just one example, consider the recent debate in congress over welfare reform. Legitimate concerns about the growing deficit and declining economic opportunity among voters were transformed by political leaders into an attack on poor women receiving public assistance. These women were vilified as "welfare queens," a rhetorical device which conjures the most virulently racist images of Black women imaginable (see chapter 4). Such manipulation is possible in a context in which institutionalized white supremacy is routinized while notions about class, gender, and sexuality go relatively unchallenged. The result is that one of the most vulnerable and disadvantaged groups in our society—poor women of color—are made to suffer even further through the elimination of government benefits while the hegemony of the current political system is reinforced. Given the abhorrent nature of the ideas discussed here and their profound political implications I would be remiss if I did not offer some consideration of strategies for combatting white supremacy.

Briefly, there are a number of strategies that have been employed to address white supremacist organizations and their discourse. Morris Dees, founder of the Southern Poverty Law Center and its subsidiary organization Klanwatch, has turned to pursuing white supremacist organizations through civil suits. While costly, this has proven to be an effective mechanism for disabling specific organizations and discontinuing a variety of ac-

135

tivities from violence to the publishing of journals such as those examined here.

There are a few relatively small organizations, such as the Northwest Coalition Against Violence based in Oregon, which attempt to address the continuing presence of white supremacist organizations in the United States. The activities of the groups usually include data collection and the staging of counter-protests against white supremacist marches. These organizations are especially important for monitoring white supremacist organizations at a regional level; however, these organizations often ebb and flow in response to white supremacist activity and do not represent anything like a nationwide movement on the part of whites against either extremist groups or institutionalized white supremacy.

Still others, rather more scholars than activists, have adopted a strategy of calling for the regulation of all "hate speech," what I refer to as white supremacist rhetoric. Advocates for this stance contend that there is nothing worth protecting in the rhetoric of these organizations and that offering them protection under the First Amendment is tacit support of white supremacy. It would be an important step toward dismantling institutionalized white supremacy if, as in Germany after World War II, the expression of such ideas would be ruled unconstitutional. While proponents make a compelling argument, there has been little success thus far in the courts with such a strategy. At the present time, there is scant support for such legislation; indeed, most (white) voters want to rescind the much more modest advances of affirmative action. Chances that either public support or legal precedent will make the outlawing of this speech a viable option seem remote at best.

The most radical opponents of white supremacy in the United States today are those who refer to themselves as "race traitors," members of what they call a "new abolition" movement. The ideas of the movement are put forward in the journal *Race Traitor*, edited by Noel Ignatiev and John Garvey. The editors and contributors argue that the most effective strategy for dismantling institutionalized white supremacy is through the abolition of the very notion of something called "the white race." While there is disagreement among members about how to abolish the white race (although there seems to be agreement on the importance of not referring to oneself as "white"), there is a shared vision that doing nothing is no longer acceptable.

It should be evident that it is simply not the case that white supremacy exists exclusively at the level of extremists. The rhetoric and images of extremist white supremacists are not, as I have demonstrated, that far removed from the way racial politics operate in presidential campaigns, for example, or get played out in popular films. Dismissing white supremacist organizations and their discourse as merely a "lunatic fringe" without any relevance to the rest of the culture maintains white privilege by removing from analytic view the similarities such discourse shares with the broader white supremacist context and by distancing the way that all whites benefit from the existence of these groups. The presence of these groups provides an "out" for whites proclaiming their racial moral innocence while obviating the need to examine institutionalized white supremacy and the way it benefits whites. Ignoring white supremacists reaffirms white supremacy; and we do so at our own peril as a society.

So, perhaps those who advocate a "new abolition" movement are correct when they assert that what we must do is not be white—resist the designation and in the process deconstruct and dismantle whiteness. I am skeptical about this though, because it is not clear what it means to *not be white*, or even to begin to move in that direction. I do agree, however, that what we can do is take responsibility for whiteness, and the way membership in that category privileges us. Whites should be resisting white supremacist discourse, in whatever form, whether in extremist publications, from political leaders, or popular culture, or out of the mouth of (pseudo) scholars who purport to have evidence of the biological inferiority of particular "races" of people. To simply do nothing is to affirm—and reap the benefits of—white privilege.

Whether or not the continued presence of these groups and the appeal of their discourse illustrates what Derrick Bell has referred to as the "permanence of racism" within the American political landscape is, I think, still an open question. However, these groups and the appeal of their rhetoric—and perhaps more importantly, the appearance of these themes in mainstream political discourse and popular culture—offer compelling evidence that we have not come as far as we would like to believe in dealing with race. And it also offers compelling evidence that "dealing with race" may not be something we can do without addressing issues of gender, sexuality, and class.

Finally, the fact that white supremacist discourse is classified as speech, or to use MacKinnon's phrase, "only words," and is therefore protected under the First Amendment is worthy of reflection. Though there is much debate about how the relationship between hate speech and hate crimes works, the fact remains that at least *some* consumers of this rhetoric *do act* on its messages with deadly consequences for their victims. We have only to recall the brutal death of Mulegetta Seraw at the hands of neo-Nazi Skinheads to be reminded of this bleak reality (Dees & Fiffer, 1993). Furthermore, if we are to truly listen to the victims of racist hate speech—that is, to those who are targets of the language, not to those who act on the language—then concern about who will or will not act on these images becomes only one serious aspect of the overall assaultiveness of the words themselves (Feagin & Sikes, 1994; Matsuda, et al., 1993). Indeed, the assaultiveness of this discourse is given still more power in a society that implicitly condones such sentiments and institutionalizes white supremacy by labeling this symbolic violence as "protected speech." If, as I suggest, this discourse is forged as a response to the perceived erosion of white male dominance and is an attempt to recreate what white, heterosexual men imagine to be a lost world of unchallenged white supremacy, then the questions before us are difficult ones. What kind of society can we imagine and, more importantly, create for ourselves? Will it be a society based on exclusion and domination—such as that in white supremacist discourse—or one, perhaps only recently glimpsed, based on equality, diversity, and inclusion?

Appendix A: Methodology

I began my study of white supremacist literature as a quantitative, content analysis project in which I planned to use a computer program to count frequencies of words. I found, however, that as I proceeded with this method I was unable to answer the theoretical questions I wanted to ask. I then turned to a method known as ethnographic content analysis, or qualitative content analysis, in which I read the publications and noted the themes which emerged while foregrounding my theoretical questions about the intersections of race, class, gender, and sexuality.

Selecting the Publications

For this project, I examined white supremacist publications from the Klanwatch collection. Klanwatch is a division of the Southern Poverty Law Center located in Montgomery, Alabama, that monitors dozens of white supremacist groups throughout the country and maintains an extensive collection of thousands of white supremacist publications. The sampling frame I used for selecting these publications was the collection inventory of Klanwatch.

In order to narrow the selection of publications to include in my sample, I considered which publications were the longest consistently published. By considering length of time published as a proxy for the relative success of publication, I could make several other inferences about the periodicals. First, I could reasonably assume that these publications had the

139

largest audiences. Since circulation figures for these publications are impossible to come by (given the clandestine nature of many of the organizations), this seemed like a sound proxy measure. I also considered these publications and the organizations behind them to be the best funded and/or managed organizations. Finally, I assumed that the journals which had been published for the longest period of time were those most successful at constructing racist ideologies. Thus, the six publications that I considered to have the largest audiences and to be the most successful publications were *The Klansman, The Torch, Thunderbolt/Truth at Last, Racial Loyalty, WAR,* and *NAAWP.*

In my sample, I included every issue of these six publications owned by Klanwatch. My data set includes 106 issues of *The Klansman,* 47 issues of *NAAWP,* 102 issues of *Thunderbolt/Truth at Last,* 33 issues of *The Torch,* 46 issues of *Racial Loyalty,* and 35 issues of *WAR,* for a total of 369 publications. (See Appendix B for a comprehensive list of all publications and issue dates, where available.) The data covered the time period 1977 through 1991. Each publication represents a distinct white supremacist organization within the movement. While the sample is not representative (organizations with less time in circulation, fewer readers, and so on, were excluded) it does represent a fairly accurate range of contemporary white supremacist movement discourse. Obviously, this is by no means a comprehensive study of the movement or its discourse (indeed, as I mention in chapter 2, my primary concern was with white supremacy broadly defined, rather than with social movement theory); there is much room and a great need for further research in this area.

Analyzing the Publications: Qualitative Content Analysis

There are many aspects of ideology that can be studied. Reeves lists several facets of ideology including genesis, ontological status, function, truth, relation to interest, and *content* of ideology which "may be studied in its own right" (Reeves, 1983:42). Content is the focus of this work. In the analysis of the content of ideology, I am primarily concerned with an interpretation of the meaning of discourse, focusing on recurrent themes and techniques of argumentation and persuasion. In the final analysis, it is meaning which is the focus:

> The content of ideology must be studied by giving an interpretation of meaning: it does not consist of studies of the genesis or behavioral effects of ideology or the motivations of social actors (Reeves, 1983:42–43).

As the above quote indicates, the goal of this research is not to understand the "effects of ideology" but rather to provide an interpretation of meaning. In this case, my goal is to understand how racist ideologies are constructed by the white supremacist movement and the ways in which gender and sexuality are integral to this construction.

I chose to study publications rather than either interview members or become a participant observer in the movement for several reasons. First of all, because what I was interested in studying was how racist ideologies are constructed, looking at groups and their publications that are directly involved in formulating racist doctrine seemed a straightforward approach. Furthermore, I was less immediately concerned with how those ideologies are appropriated by movement members, so direct contact with group members seemed superfluous. Second, I contend that examining white supremacist literature is a valid measure of a particular (and extreme) form of racist ideology which is sometimes difficult to examine in the contemporary United States. One of the difficulties of accurately studying racism in the current context is that we live in an era in which openly expressed racist sentiment has become socially unacceptable (Bobo, 1988; Feagin & Feagin, 1986; Jhally & Lewis, 1992; Kleugel & Smith, 1986; Sears, 1988). I chose this method because there is little, if any, hesitation within white supremacist publications about articulating overt racist ideologies.

Here, I utilized *qualitative*, or ethnographic, content analysis to explore the ideology of the white supremacist movement. In contrast to quantitative content analysis, which emphasizes counting words for the purpose of generating frequencies and testing hypotheses, ethnographic content analysis emphasizes textual analysis for the purpose of generating theory.

The procedure for ethnographic content analysis can best be understood as a two-stage process (Altheide, 1987; Ely, et al., 1991; Fields, 1988). In stage one of this process, I noted words, images, and recurring themes in the publications. This preliminary reading and the early "field" notes were useful to me as I moved on to stage two. Stage two was much longer and included most of the analysis. This stage included choosing a unit of analysis; developing categories and a system for noting them; textual, visual, composition analysis; and finally, explanation.

I chose articles as my unit of analysis because I was interested in examining broad themes within the publications. In developing categories, I began to focus on the representations of different racial groups, i.e., whites, Blacks, and Jews. Then, I noted the way that men and women within those groups were represented, so that categories such as white men, white women, Black men, and Black women began to emerge. I then noted particular themes that began to materialize within each of

141

these categories and the ways those representations differed or were similar to those in other categories. For example, within the category "white men," certain themes were repeated, such as the characterization of white men as soldiers or racial warriors. Thus, "white men-warriors" became a useful category.

In order to record which publications I had read and the categories that applied to those publications I developed a note-taking system. The system included writing the publication's name, year, and issue number at the top of the page, noting the relevant article and any significant text on the right two-thirds of the page, and noting the categories the article fit on the left third of the page.

As I went through the publications, I also conducted textual, visual, and compositional analyses. Textual analysis involves asking what messages are being conveyed in the article. Visual analysis is concerned with the messages in the photos, illustrations, and cartoons. Compositional analysis is concerned with the way the textual and visual components are arranged. In other words, compositional analysis examines the juxtapositions of textual and visual arrangements, focusing on the appearance, recurrence, or disappearance of particular patterns. The final portion of stage two is explanation. Here I tried to understand how this research explains, supports, or contradicts the theoretical discussions laid out in earlier chapters.

Discourse Analysis

As I use it here, discourse analysis refers to a methodology which, rather than examining syntax or sentence structure, looks at words, images, and themes in juxtaposition to each other and most importantly to the broader social, cultural, and political context. Thus, while ethnographic content analysis involved the initial step of laying out the themes in white supremacist rhetoric, discourse analysis went the further step of layering the analysis of those themes with differing interpretations (see, for example, Kellner, 1990). This layering often entailed making the linkages between extremist expressions of white supremacy and mainstream discussions of race, class, gender, and sexuality explicit.

The objective of such analysis is deconstruction on a number of fronts. At one level, the purpose is to expose and simultaneously struggle against the rhetorical mechanisms used in white supremacist discourse; for instance, the construction of "whiteness" relies on particular notions of gender and sexuality. The more difficult work of discourse analysis lay in the process of deconstructing white supremacist ideology and its pernicious and insidious logic. For example, the rhetoric about Black men's inherent criminality seems, at first glance, a relatively easy notion to resist as a rather blatantly white supremacist construct. However, it was after a prominent scholar in criminology read some of my work and objected to it by saying, ". . . but Black men *are* more criminal," that I realized that the real work of discourse analysis is in deconstructing the categories themselves and setting out, often in excruciating detail, how such ideas are false, are indeed, "white lies."

Ethical and Political Considerations

As with any project that attempts to explore systems of dominance and repression, there are some important ethical and political issues that must be examined. While still formulating my research design, I considered the possibility of doing interviews with members (or becoming a member myself) of white supremacist organizations, and this presented me with a host of ethical dilemmas. Interviewing or traditional ethnography both required that I represent myself to respondents or participants as an "objective," or at the very least impartial, social science observer. Other scholars who have conducted interviews with white supremacists have noted that the participation of respondents relied on the premise of shared assumptions (Aho, 1990; Blee, 1991). Such a representation lay at the heart of my ethical conundrum because I am not "impartial" when it comes to white supremacy; thus, holding myself out as disinterested would require a deception of the respondents which I consider unethical. In addition, in conducting interviews or an ethnography in which I combined a claim to no particular opinion regarding white supremacy, with my social science credentials I ran the risk of lending credibility to a movement whose aims I fundamentally oppose.

In some ways, choosing to examine white supremacist publications (rather than interviewing real live human beings) helped me avoid this predicament and made it somewhat easier to negotiate. However, my decision to examine the publications did not resolve ethical questions because there were also ethical considerations in selecting a source for the publications. In the early stages of this research I secured a mailing address away from my home and got on the mailing list of the white supremacist group Christian Identity under a pseudonym. (I heard the address given on a "Sally Jessy Raphael" show about the group and used the pseudonym "Jean L. Finch," after the main character in *To Kill a Mockingbird*, by Harper Lee.) I received *The Torch* for several months afterward free of charge, then began receiving solicitations for funds from the group. It was at this point that I decided to remove my name from the mailing list and seek alternative sources of publications. By leaving my name, or pseudonym, on a mailing list and even more so, by sending in donations to receive more publications, I would have been supporting the white supremacist movement. I decided instead to support one of the half-dozen or so organizations that monitor these groups. Klanwatch has the most extensive archive of publications and they gave me extraordinary access to these archives. Using the Klanwatch archives allowed me to obtain a large sample of white supremacist publications without lending any support, or even the appearance of support, to the movement or its aims.

Ethical concerns surrounding issues of empathy with white supremacists and their ideologies were ultimately much more difficult to confront. Within the social sciences, there has been much debate about whether the role of the researcher is to strive for objective measures of social facts or to pursue the goal of *verstehen*, that is, an empathic understanding of the research "subjects." This is an approach that feminist scholars, myself included, have embraced and pointed to as an avenue for changing the social order while studying it. Most frequently, this has been appropriated by feminist scholars studying women's lives as a stratagem for taking women and their experiences seriously. In practice this becomes problematic when the subjects of research hold views that are odious to the researcher. On the one hand, I wanted to gain an empathetic understanding of how those who subscribe to the white supremacist ideology view the world; on the other hand, I did not want to embrace white supremacy, even momentarily. The dilemma, then, was (and continues to be) between my empathy for them as fellow human beings and my deep abhorrence of their views, between my stance as a scholar and my reaction as an activist committed to social change.

My response to this impasse was a postmodern one, seeing my work as simply the relation between the researcher and the researched by positioning myself—my identity and my standpoint—in relation to the text, as I did in the discussion at the beginning of the book about epistemology, whiteness, and sexual politics. The choice of a postmodern stance seems the most appropriate solution. I do not think that even the most ardent supporters of "objective" social science can make a convincing case for moral neutrality when it comes to avowed white supremacists or their rhetoric. If the goal in studying these ideologies is to understand the ways our institutions and cultural, as well as individual, practices reinforce and sustain them, then I contend that it is not possible to do this from a "value-free" stance. Whatever the particular methodology we use as sociologists, it is incumbent upon us as researchers to examine the implications of our methodological choice for dismantling, rather than sustaining, systems of domination.

Appendix B: Publication Inventory*
(n=369)

The Klansman 1976–1992

Year	Month	Issue
1976	September	#7
1978	February	#26
1978	July	#31
1978	September	#33
1978	October	#34
1979	January	#37
1979	March	#39
1979	May	#41
1979	July	#43
1979	August	#44
1979	September	#45
1979	October	#46
1980	January	#49
1980	February	#50
1980	April	#52
1980	June	#54

* NOTE: The Publications listed here reflect those that the Klanwatch Archive, and now I, actually have in hand. How consistently—or accurately—issues are numbered and published varied between (and within) publications. Inconsistencies and inaccuracies in numbering are the responsibliity of each publisher.

1980	November	#59
1980	December	#60
1981	February	#62
1981	April	#64
1981	May	#65
1981	June	#66
1981	July	#67
1981	August	#68
1981	September	#69
1981	October	#70
1981	November/December	#71
1982	February	#73
1982	June	#77
1982	August	#79
1982	September	#80
1982	November	#82
1982	December	#83
1983	January	#84
1983	March	#86
1983	April	#87
1983	May	#88
1983	June	#89
1983	July	#90
1983	August	#91
1983	September	#92
1983	October	#93
1983	November	#94
1983	December	#95
1984	January	#96
1984	February	#97
1984	March	#98
1984	April	#99
1984	May	#100
1984	June	#101
1984	July	#102
1984	August	#103
1984	September	#104
1984	October	#105

1984	November	#106
1984	December	#107
1984	January	#108
1985	February	#109
1985	April/May	#111
		#112
1985	June/July	#113
		#114
1985	August/September	#115
		#116
1985	October	#117
1985	November/December	#118
		#119
1986	January	#120
1986	February/March/April	#121
1986	May/June	#122
1986	July/August	#123
1986	September/October	#124
1986	November/December	#125
1986	Special Education	—
1987	January/February	#126
1987	March/April	#127
1987	May/June	#128
1987	Spring Special Education	—
1987	July/August	#129
1987	September/October	#130
1987	November/December	#131
1988	January/February	#132
1988	March/April	#133
1988	May/June	#134
1988	July/August	#135
1988	September/October	#136
1988	November/December	#137
1989	January/February	#138
1989	March/April	#139
1989	May/June	#140
1989	July/August	#141

1989	September/October	#142
1989	November/December	#143
1990	January/February	#144
1990	May/June	#145
1990	July/August	#146
1990	September/October	#147
1990	November/December	#148
1991	January/February	#149
1991	March/April	#150
1991	May/June	#151
1991	July/August	#152
1991	September/October	#153
1991	November/December	#154
1992	January/February	#155
1992	March/April	#157

SUBTOTAL: 106

NAAWP, 1980–1991

Year	Month	Issue
1982	—	#1
—	—	#1
1980	—	#2
1980	—	#5
1981	—	#6
1981	—	#7
1982	—	#13
1982	—	#15
1982	—	#18
1982	—	#19
1982	—	#20
1982	—	#21
1982	—	#22
1982	—	#23
1983	—	#26

1983	—	#27
1984	[Special Issue]	—
1984	—	#28
1984	—	#29
1984	—	#31
1984	—	#32
1984	—	#33
—	—	#34
—	—	#35
—	—	#36
[rec'd 1986 October]		#37
—	—	#38
—	—	#39
—	—	#41
—	—	#42
—	—	#43
—	—	#48
[rec'd 1987 December]		#49
[rec'd 1988 February]		#50
[rec'd 1988 May]		#51
[rec'd 1988 July]		#52
[rec'd 1988 October]		#53
[rec'd 1988 December]		#54
[rec'd 1989 May]		#55
—	—	#56
—	—	#58
—	—	#59
[rec'd 1990 November]		Special Issue
[rec'd 1991 February]		#61
[rec'd 1991 May]		#62
[rec'd 1991 August]		#63
[rec'd 1991 October]		#64–1
[rec'd 1991 December]		#64–2

SUBTOTAL: 47

Thunderbolt/Truth at Last, 1978–c.1992

Year	Month	Issue
1978	August	#232
1979	December	#248
1980	April	#252
1980	July	#255
1980	August	#256
1980	September	#257
1980	October	#258
1980	November	#259
1980	December	#260
1981	January	#261
1981	February	#262
1981	March	#263
1981	April	#264
1981	May	#265
1981	June	#266
1981	July	#267
1981	August	#268
1981	October	#270
1981	November	#271
1981	December	#272
1982	January	#273
1982	February	#274
1982	March	#275
1982	April	#276
1982	May	#277
1982	July	#279
1982	September	#281
1982	October	#282
1982	November	#283
1982	December	#284
1983	January	#285
1983	March	#286
1983	April	#287
1983	May	#288
1983	June	#289

1983	July	#290
1983	August	#291
1983	September	#292
1983	October	#293
1984	January	#294
1984	February	#295
1984	—	#297
1984	—	#298
1984	August	#299
—	—	#300
—	—	#301
—	—	#302
—	—	#303

[c.1985—years/months not listed after thispoint]

—	—	#304
—	—	#305
—	—	#306
—	—	#307
—	—	#308
—	—	#309

[c.1986]

—	—	#310
—	—	#311
—	—	#312
—	—	#313
—	—	#314
—	—	#315

[c.1987]

—	—	#316
—	—	#317
—	—	#318
—	—	#319
[rec'd 1987 September]		#320
—	—	#321

[c.1988]

—	—	#322
—	—	#326
—	—	#327

[rec'd 1988 August]	#328
— —	#329

[changes to *Truth at Last* at this point]

[c.1989]

— —	#330
— —	#331
[rec'd 1989 March]	#332
[rec'd 1989 April]	#333
[rec'd 1989 May]	#334
[rec'd 1989 July]	#335
[rec'd 1989 August]	#336
— —	#337
— —	#338
— —	#339
— —	#340

[c.1990]

— —	#341
— —	#342
— —	#343
[rec'd October 1990]	#344
[rec'd November 1990]	#345
[rec'd January 1991]	#346

[c.1991]

— —	#347
— —	#348
[rec'd 1991 May]	#349
[rec'd 1991 July]	#350
— —	#351
[rec'd 1991August]	Special Issue
[rec'd 1991 October]	#352
[rec'd 1991 December]	#353

SUBTOTAL: 102

The Torch, 1977–1991

Year	Month	Issue
1977	March	Vol. 9, #2
1977	July	Vol. 9, #3
1979	October	Vol. 10, #4
1980	January	Vol. 11, #5
1980	August	Vol. 11, #7
1981	January	Vol. 12, #8
1981	July	Vol. 12, #9
	[no vol. # listed after this]	
1982	July	#110
1982	September	#112
1982	October	#113
1982	November	#114
1982	December/January	#115
1983	—	#116
1983	—	#117
1983	—	#118
1984	January	#120
1984	March	#121
1984	June	#122
1984	July	#123
1984	September	#124
1985	April	#125
1985	May	#126
1985	August	#127
1985	—	#128
1986	March	#128
1988	June	#129
1989	[rec'd March]	#131
1989	July	#134
1990	April	#136
1990	[rec'd October]	#137

| 1991 | [rec'd April] | #138 |
| 1991 | [rec'd October] | #140 |

SUBTOTAL: 33

Racial Loyalty, 1984–1992

Year	Month	Issue
1984	January	#8
1985	February	#21
1986	November	#37
1987	February	#38
1987	June	#39
1988	July	#40
1988	August	#41
1988	September	#42
1988	October	#43
1988	November	#44
1988	December	#45
1989	January	#46
1989	February	#47
1989	March	#48
1989	April	#49
1989	May	#50
1989	June	#51
1989	July	#52
1989	August	#53
1989	September	#54
1989	October	#55
1989	December	#56
1990	February	#57
1990	April	#58
1990	May	#59
1990	June	#60
1990	July	#61
1990	August	#62
1990	September	#63

1990	October	#64
1990	November	#65
1990	December	#66
1991	January	#67
1991	February	#68
1991	April	#69
1991	May	#70
1991	June	#71
1991	August	#72
1991	September	#73
1991	October	#74
1991	November	#75
1991	December	#76
1992	January	#77
1992	February	#78
1992	March	#79
1992	May	#80

SUBTOTAL: 46

WAR, 1984–1992

Year	Month	Issue #
[1984]	—	Vol. 3, #4
	—	Vol. 3, #5
1985	—	Vol. 4, #1
1985	[rec'd April]	Vol. 4, #2
1985	—	Vol. 4, #3
1985	—	Vol. 4, #4
1985	—	Vol. 4, #5
	Special Issue	
1986	—	Vol. 5, #1
1986	—	Vol. 5, #2
1986	—	Vol. 5, #3
1987	—	Vol. 6, #1
1987	—	Vol. 6, #2
1987	—	Vol. 6, #3

1987	—	Vol. 6, #4
1987	—	Vol. 6, #5
1987	—	Vol. 6, #6
1988	—	Vol. 7, #1
1988	—	Vol. 7, #2
1988	—	Vol. 7, #3
1988	—	Vol. 7, #4
1988	—	Vol. 7, #5
1988	—	Vol. 7, #6
1989	—	Vol. 8, #1
1989	—	Vol. 8, #2
1989	[rec'd August]	Vol. 8, #3
1989	—	Vol. 8, #4
1989	Double Issue	Vol. 8, #5 & #6
1990	—	Vol. 9, #1
1990	—	Vol. 9, #2
1990	—	Vol. 9, #3
1990	—	Vol. 9, #4
1990	—	Vol. 9, #5
1991	—	Vol. 10, #1
1991	—	Vol. 10, #2
1992	[rec'd April]	Vol. 11, #1
SUBTOTAL:	35	

Notes

Chapter 2:   White Supremacist Movement(s) in a
White Supremacist Context

1. The regions where the Klan drew the most members shared the fact that they had few minorities and were overwhelmingly white and Protestant.

Chapter 3:   Visions of Masculinity, Glimpses of Feminity:
White Men and White Women

1. Some groups, like those represented here by the *Thunderbolt*, along with those of Christian Identity seen in *The Torch*, and the Ku Klux Klan seen in *The Klansman*, do embrace a fundamentalist, Protestant version of Christianity; while others, such as the neo-Nazis and Skinheads represented by *WAR*, eschew notions of "God" altogether and instead draw on pagan imagery. Creators, represented here by *Racial Loyalty*, subscribe to a view which equates any form of Christianity with Judaism and thus rejects all religion and ideas of "God." Instead, Creators hold that the white race *is* their religion.

2. Tom Metzger, the founder of *WAR*, works as a television repairman, a solidly working-class occupation.

3. Ben Klassen, founder of The Church of the Creator and publisher of *Racial Loyalty*, was a college-educated state legislator and multi-millionaire real-estate developer. David Duke, founder of the NAAWP and publisher of the *NAAWP News*, also has a college degree and served as a state

legislator before his almost successful bid for Governor of Louisiana. Indeed, the white supremacist movement, in its shift from hoods and robes to suits and ties, has taken on a decidedly upwardly mobile hue. Klassen and Duke's organizations are two factions of the fastest-growing elements of the white supremacist movement. Even John Metzger, the son of working-class white supremacist Tom Metzger, is pursuing a college degree in California and has founded the "White Student Union," an organization designed to "stand up for the rights of white male students who cannot get jobs after graduation" (*WAR*, special issue, 1985, p. 2).

4. Interestingly, this is one of the few appearances in white supremacist discourse of Hispanics as racialized Others. Most often, it is African Americans and Jews who are featured as the hypervisible racialized Others. Hispanics, Asian Americans, and any people not sanctioned as "white" are racialized as "Mud" people.

5. The drawing is a response to the controversy in several Southern states over the use of the stars and bars in state flags. Many Blacks have protested the use of the symbol as a vestige of a racist past, while many whites contend that the flag represents a proud heritage.

6. I will address this connection between race and homosexuality in more detail in chapters 4 and 5.

7. White supremacists' response to Vanessa Williams's rise and subsequent fall as Miss America will be discussed in more detail in chapter 4.

8. The organization was defunct by 1991.

9. The doctor, it should be noted, in all four panels of the cartoon is Jewish. This is, of course, not coincidental. Within white supremacist discourse, abortion is part of a genocidal plot against "middle and low income whites, perpetrated by Jewish abortionists," (*WAR*, vol. 3, no. 4, p. 2). I address this issue in more detail in chapter 5. The importance given to abortion by the white supremacist movement is further illustrated by Ralph Forbes's lawsuit against the University of Arkansas Medical Science Hospital to stop all pregnancy termination procedures.

10. I will address O. J. Simpson in more detail in the following chapter.

Chapter 4: "Rapists," "Welfare Queens," and Vanessa Williams: Black Men and Black Women

1. The language that will unite the white race, according to Creators.

2. The term "racist" is not being used in a perjorative sense here, but rather in the white supremacist usage as "racially aware."

3. Vanessa Williams was the first Black Miss America, crowned in 1984; she then was forced to resign amid scandal. Suzette Charles, also a Black

woman, was the first runner-up and her replacement. I will discuss this scandal in more depth later in this chapter.

4. Along with the racially unidentifiable woman in bed with him.

5. This article appeared before Barry became embroiled in scandal.

6. Duke justified his appearance in *Hustler* to *NAAWP* readers by saying that while the magazine "can be pretty vile and pornographic . . . it is read by millions of two-fisted white working men and many college students," presumably Duke's target audience.

7. Some evidence suggests that this is not true of all white supremacists, however. Bill Stanton, former director of Klanwatch, writes, "In the course of our various investigations into the Klan we ran across several KKK members who admitted having had sexual relations with nonwhites, suggesting that it was not that rare an occurrence" (Stanton, 1991, p. 231).

8. Beauty pageants themselves are not problematic, as long as they unequivocally confirm ideals of white feminine beauty. *The Klansman* ran an article praising a white Miss America, Susan Akin, because it was reported that her father and grandfather were Klan members. Akin was lauded as a "beautiful, blonde . . . product of the kind of the racial separation the Klan teaches" *(The Klansman,* no. 118–19, 1985, p. 4).

9. As a solution, an interested reader of *NAAWP* suggested a "Miss NAAWP Pageant."

Chapter 5: "ZOG," Bankers, and "Bull Dyke" Feminists: Jewish Men and Jewish Women

1. In 1913, in Marietta, Georgia, Leo Frank, a Jewish man, was accused of raping and murdering thirteen-year-old Mary Phagan. Frank was tried, convicted, and sentenced to death. Before the case could be appealed or the sentence carried out, a mob of Cobb County residents, calling themselves "The Knights of Mary Phagan," kidnapped Frank from the state prison and lynched him. Legal scholars and historians have long since debated Frank's guilt or innocence; white supremacists have not.

Bibliography

Adorno, T. W., et al. 1964. *The Authoritarian Personality.* New York: John Wiley & Sons.

Aho, James. 1990. *The Politics of Righteousness: Idaho Christian Patriotism.* Seattle: University of Washington Press.

Albert, Michael, et al. 1986. *Liberating Theory.* Boston: South End Press.

Alexander, Charles C. 1965. *The Ku Klux Klan in the Southwest.* Lexington: University of Kentucky Press.

Allen, Theodore W. 1994. *The Invention of the White Race. Volume One: Racial Oppression and Social Control.* London: Verso.

Allport, Gordon W. 1954. *The Nature of Prejudice.* Reading, MA: Addison Wesley.

Altheide, David L. 1987. "Ethnographic Content Analysis." *Qualitative Sociology* 10, 1 (Spring):65–77.

Applebome, Peter. 1993. "Skinhead Violence Grows, Experts Say." *New York Times,* 18 July 1993, A11.

———. 1991. "Fearing Duke, Voters in Louisiana Hand Democrat Fourth Term." *New York Times,* 18 November, A1.

Banton, Michael P. 1977. *The Idea of Race.* London: Tavistock.

Beck, Evelyn. 1992. "From 'KIKE' to 'JAP': How Misogyny, Anti-Semitism, and Racism Construct the 'Jewish American Princess.' " In *Race, Class and Gender: An Anthology,* edited by Margaret L. Andersen and Patricia Hill Collins, 88–95. Belmont, CA.: Wadsworth Publishing.

Bell, Derrick. 1992. *Faces at the Bottom of the Well.* New York: Basic Books.

Biddis, Michael D. 1970. *Father of Racist Ideology: The Social and Political Thought of Count Gobineau.* New York: Weybright and Talley.

Blauner, Bob. 1989. *Black Lives, White Lives: Three Decades of Race Relations in America.* Berkeley: University of California Press.

Blee, Kathleen. 1991a. "Women in the 1920s Ku Klux Klan Movement." *Feminist Studies* 1 (Spring):57–77.

———. 1991b. *Women of the Klan: Racism and Gender in the 1920s.* Berkeley: University of California Press.

Bobo, Lawrence. 1988. "Group Conflict, Prejudice, and the Paradox of Contemporary Racial Attitudes." In *Eliminating Racism: Profiles in Controversy,* edited by Phyllis A. Katz and Dalmas A. Taylor, 85–114. New York: Plenum Press.

Bordo, Susan. 1993. *Unbearable Weight.* Berkeley: University of California Press.

Bowser, Benjamin P., and Raymond G. Hunt, eds. 1981. *Impacts of Racism on White Americans.* Beverly Hills, CA: Sage.

Brittan, Arthur, and Mary Maynard. 1984. *Sexism, Racism and Oppression.* London: Blackwell.

Brod, Harry, ed. 1988. *Mensch among Men: Explorations in Jewish Masculinity.* Freedom, Calif.: Crossing Press.

Burawoy, Michael, et al. 1991. *Ethnography Unbound: Power and Resistance in the Modern Metropolis.* Berkeley: University of California Press.

Carby, Hazel. 1987a. *Reconstructing Womanhood.* Oxford: Oxford University Press.

———. 1987b. "Slave and Mistress: Ideologies of Womanhood under Slavery." In *Reconstructing Womanhood: The Emergence of the Afro-American Woman Novelist.* New York: Oxford University Press.

———. 1982. "White Woman Listen! Black Feminism and the Boundaries of Sisterhood." In *The Empire Strikes Back: Race and Racism in 70s Britain,* edited by Center for Contemporary Studies, 212–35. London: Hutchinson.

Chalmers, David M. 1987. *Hooded Americanism: The History of the Ku Klux Klan.* Durham: Duke University Press.

Clawson, Mary Ann. 1989. *Constructing Brotherhood: Class, Gender, and Fraternalism.* Princeton: Princeton University Press.

Collins, Patricia Hill. 1990. *Black Feminist Thought: Knowledge, Consciousness, and the Politics of Empowerment.* Boston: Unwin Hyman.

Condor, Susan. 1988. " 'Race Stereotype' and Racist Discourse." *Text* 8:69–89.

Connell, R.W. 1987. *Gender and Power: Society, the Person and Sexual Politics.* Stanford: Stanford University Press.

Cox, Oliver Cromwell. 1948. *Caste, Class and Race: A Study in Social Dynamics.* New York: Monthly Review Press.

D'Emilio, John, and Estelle B. Freeman. 1988. *Intimate Matters: A History of Sexuality in America.* New York: Harper & Row.

Davis, Angela Y. 1983. *Women, Race and Class.* New York: Vintage.

Davis, Lenwood G., and Janet L. Sims-Wood, eds. 1984. *The Ku Klux Klan: A Bibliography.* Westport, CT: Greenwood Press.

Dees, Morris, and Steve Fiffer. 1993. *Hate on Trial.* New York: Villard Books.

Diesing, Paul. 1971. *Patterns of Discovery in the Social Sciences.* Chicago: Aldine Atherton.

Dijk, T. A. van. 1987. *Communicating Racism: Ethnic Prejudice in Thought and Talk.* Newbury Park, CA: Sage.

Dill, Bonnie Thornton. 1984. "The Dialectics of Black Womanhood." *Signs* 4 (Spring):543–55.

———. 1983. "Race, Class and Gender: Prospects for an All-Inclusive Sisterhood." *Feminist Studies* 9 (Spring):131–50.

Dinnerstein, Leonard. 1994. *Anti-Semitism in America.* New York: Beacon Press.

Dixon, Thomas Jr. 1905. *The Clansman.* New York: Dunlap.

Dobratz, Betty A., and Stephanie Shanks-Meile. 1988. "The Contemporary Ku Klux Klan and the American Nazi Party: A Comparison to American Populism at the Turn of the Century." *Humanity & Society* 12 (1):20–50.

Donald, James, and Stuart Hall, eds. 1986. *Politics and Ideology.* Philadelphia: Open University Press.

Drake, St. Clair. 1987–1990. *Black Folk Here and There.* 2 vols. Los Angeles: Center for Afro-American Studies, University of California.

Du Bois, W. E. Burghardt. 1939. *Black Folk Then and Now: An Essay in the History and Sociology of the Negro Race.* New York: Henry Holt and Company.

Dye, Thomas R. 1983. *Who's Running America?* Englewood Cliffs, NJ: Prentice-Hall.

Easlea, Brian. 1981. *Science and Sexual Oppression: Patriarchy's Confrontation with Woman and Nature.* London: Weidenfeld & Nicolson.

Eisenstein, Hester. 1983. *Contemporary Feminist Thought.* Boston: G. K. Hall.

Ely, Margot, et al., eds. 1991. *Doing Qualitative Research: Circles within Circles.* London: The Falmer Press.

Essed, Philomena. 1991. *Understanding Everyday Racism: An Interdisciplinary Theory.* Newbury Park, CA: Sage.

Fanon, Franz. 1967. *Black Skin, White Masks.* Translated by Charles Lam Markmann. New York: Grove Weidenfeld.

Feagin, Joe R., and Melvin P. Sikes. 1994. *Living with Racism: The Black Middle-Class Experience.* Boston: Beacon Press.

———. and Clairece Booher Feagin. 1993. *Racial and Ethnic Relations*, 4th ed. Englewood Cliffs, NJ: Prentice Hall.

———. 1986. *Discrimination American Style: Institutional Racism and Sexism*. Malabar, FL: Krieger Publishing.

Ferber, Abby. *The Ultimate Abomination: Race, Gender, and White Supremacy*. New York: New York University Press (forthcoming).

Fields, Echo E. 1988. "Qualitative Content Analysis of Television News: Systematic Techniques." *Qualitative Sociology* 11, 1 (Fall):183–189.

Flynn, Kevin, and Gary Gerhardt. 1989. *The Silent Brotherhood: Inside America's Racist Underground*. New York: Free Press.

Franklin, Clyde. 1984. *The Changing Definition of Masculinity*. New York: Plenum.

Frederickson, George M. 1981. *White Supremacy: A Comparative Study in American and South African History*. Oxford: Oxford University Press.

———. 1971. *The Black Image in the White Mind: The Debate on Afro-American Character and Destiny, 1817–1914*. New York: Harper & Row.

Gilman, Sander L. 1985. *Difference and Pathology: Stereotypes of Sexuality, Race and Madness*. Ithaca, NY: Cornell University Press.

Gilroy, Paul. 1987. *"Ain't No Black in the Union Jack": The Cultural Politics of Race and Nation*. London: Hutchinson.

Glaser, Barney G., and Anselm L. Strauss. 1967. *The Discovery of Grounded Theory: Strategies for Qualitative Research*. Chicago: Aldine.

Glock, Charles Y., and Rodney Stark. 1966. *Christian Beliefs and Anti-Semitism*. New York: Harper & Row.

Goldsby, Jackie. 1993. "Queen for 307 Days: Looking B(l)ack at Vanessa Williams and the Sex Wars." In *Sisters, Sexperts, Queers: Beyond the Lesbian Nation*, edited by Arlene Stein, 11–129. New York: Plume.

Gossett, Thomas F. 1963. *Race: The History of an Idea in America*. Dallas: Southern Methodist University Press.

Gramsci, Antonio. 1971. *Selections from the Prison Notebooks*, edited by G. Nowell Smith and Q. Hoare. New York: International Publications.

Grossberg, Laurence, ed. 1988. *Marxism and the Interpretation of Culture*. Urbana: University of Illinois Press.

Hacker, Andrew. 1992. *Two Nations: Separate, Hostile and Unequal*. New York: Scribners.

Hall, Jacquelyn Dowd. 1983. "The Mind that Burns in Each Body: Women, Rape and Racial Violence." In *Powers of Desire: The Politics of Sexuality*, edited by Ann Snitow, Christine Stansell, and Sharon Thompson, 328–49. New York: Monthly Review Press.

———. 1979. *Revolt against Chivalry: Jessie Daniel Ames and the Women's Campaign Against Lynching*. New York: Columbia University Press.

Hall, Stuart. 1982. "The Rediscovery of 'Ideology': Return of the Repressed in Media Studies." In *Culture, Society and the Media*, edited by Michael Gurevitch, et al., 56–90. London: Methuen.

―――. 1986. "Gramsci's Relevance for the Study of Race and Ethnicity." *Journal of Communication Inquiry* 10, 2 (Summer):5–27.

Harper, Suzanne. 1993. "Talking about Hate: Television Talk Shows and Hate Groups." Paper presented at the 23rd Annual Popular Culture Association Meetings, April 1993, New Orleans, Louisiana.

―――. 1990. "Lynching: Race, Class and Gender Oppression." Unpublished Master's Thesis, University of Texas, Austin.

Hernton, Calvin C. 1965. *Sex and Racism in America*. New York: Doubleday.

Himmelstein, Jerry. 1983. "Rhetorical Continuities in the Politics of Race: The Closed Society Revisited." *Southern Speech Communication Journal* 48:153–66.

hooks, bell. 1992. *Black Looks: Race and Representation*. Boston: South End Press.

―――. 1984. *Feminist Theory: From Margin to Center*. Boston: South End Press.

Hull, Gloria T., and Beverly Smith, eds. 1981. *All the Women Are White, All the Blacks Are Men, But Some of Us Are Brave: Black Women's Studies*. Old Westbury, NY: The Feminist Press.

Hurtado, Aida. 1989. "Relating to Privilege: Seduction and Rejection in the Subordination of White Women and Women of Color." *Signs* 14 (4):833–55.

Jeffords, Susan. 1989. *The Remasculinization of America: Gender and the Vietnam War*. Bloomington: University of Indiana Press.

Jhally, Sut, and Justin Lewis. 1992. *Enlightened Racism: The Cosby Show, Audiences, and the Myth of the American Dream*. Boulder, CO: Westview Press.

Jordan, Winthrop. 1977. *White Over Black: American Attitudes Toward the Negro, 1550–1812*. New York: Norton.

―――. 1974. *The White Man's Burden*. Chapel Hill: University of North Carolina Press.

Katz, Phyllis A., and Dalmas A. Taylor, eds. 1989. *Eliminating Racism: Profiles in Controversy*. New York: Plenum Press.

Katz, William Loren. 1986. *The Invisible Empire: The Ku Klux Klan Impact on History*. New York: Open Hand Publishing.

Keller, Evelyn Fox. 1985. *Reflections on Gender and Science*. New Haven, CT: Yale University Press.

Klanwatch. 1992. *Annual Report*. Montgomery, Alabama: The Klanwatch Project of the Southern Poverty Law Center.

Kluegel, James R., and Eliot R. Smith. 1986. *Beliefs about Inequality: American's Views of What Is and What Ought to Be.* New York: A. De Gruyter.

Koonz, Claudia. 1987. *Mothers in the Fatherland: Women, Family Life, and Nazi Politics.* New York: St. Martin's Press.

Kovel, Joel. 1970. *White Racism: A Psychohistory.* New York: Pantheon.

Kushner, Tony, and Kenneth Lunn, eds. 1989. *Traditions of Intolerance: Historical Perspectives on Fascism and Race Discourse in Britain.* Manchester: Manchester University Press.

Langer, Elinor. 1990. "The American Neo-Nazi Movement Today." *The Nation,* 16–23 July, 82–108.

Lester, John C. 1905. *Ku Klux Klan: Its Origin, Growth and Disbandment.* Nashville, TN: Wheeler, Osborn & Duckworth.

Lewontin, R. C., Steven Rose, and Leon J. Kamin. 1984. *Not in Our Genes: Biology, Ideology, and Human Nature.* New York: Pantheon Books.

Lipset, Seymour Martin, and Earl Raab. 1970. *Politics of Unreason: Right-Wing Extremism in America, 1790–1970.* New York: Harper & Row.

MacKinnon, Catherine A. 1993. *Only Words.* Cambridge, MA.: Harvard University Press.

———. 1989. *Toward a Feminist Theory of the State.* Cambridge, MA: Harvard University Press.

Mannheim, Karl. 1985. *Ideology and Utopia.* Translated by Louis Wirth and Edward Shils. San Diego: Harcourt Brace Jovanovich.

Matsuda, Mari J., Charles R. Lawrence III, Richard Delgado, and Kimberle Williams Crenshaw. 1993. *Words that Wound: Critical Race Theory, Assaultive Speech and the First Amendment.* Boulder, CO: Westview Press.

McLemore, S. Dale. 1980. *Racial and Ethnic Relations in America.* Boston: Allyn and Bacon.

Mecklin, John Moffatt. 1924. *The Ku Klux Klan: A Study of the American Mind.* New York: Harcourt, Brace and Company.

Mercer, Colin. 1986. "Fascist Ideology." In *Politics and Ideology,* edited by James Donald and Stuart Hall, 208–39. Philadelphia: Open University Press.

Mills, C. Wright. 1959. *The Sociological Imagination.* Oxford: Oxford University Press.

Moore, Leonard J. 1991. *Citizen Klansmen: The Ku Klux Klan in Indiana, 1921–1928.* Chapel Hill: University of North Carolina Press.

Morrison, Toni. 1992. *Playing in the Dark: Whiteness and the Literary Imagination.* Cambridge, MA: Harvard University Press.

Mosse, George L. 1978. *Toward the Final Solution: A History of European Racism.* New York: Harper & Row.

Murray, Charles. 1984. *Losing Ground.* New York: Basic Books.

———— and Richard J. Herrstein. 1994. *The Bell Curve*. New York: The Free Press.

Myrdal, Gunnar. 1944. *An American Dilemma: Vol. 2: The Negro Social Structure*. New York: Harper and Brothers.

Omi, Michael. 1990. "The 'New' Racism: Contemporary Racial Ideologies." Paper presented at the Eighty-fifth Annual Meeting of the American Sociological Association. Washington, D.C., August 11–15.

———— and Howard Winant. 1986. *Racial Formation in the United States from the 1960s to the 1980s*. New York: Routledge & Kegan Paul.

Potter, Jonathan, and Margaret Wetherell. 1988. "Accomplishing Attitudes: Race and Evaluation in Racist Discourse." *Text* 8:51–68.

Reeves, Frank. 1983. *British Racial Discourse: A Study of British Political Discourse about Race and Race-related Matters*. Cambridge: Cambridge University Press.

Ridgeway, James. 1990. *Blood in the Face: The Ku Klux Klan, Aryan Nations, Nazi Skinheads, and the Rise of a New White Culture*. New York: Thunder's Mouth Press.

Roediger, David R. 1991. *The Wages of Whiteness: Race and the Making of the American Working Class*. New York: Verso.

Rollins, Judith. 1985. *Between Women: Domestics and Their Employers*. Philadelphia: Temple University Press.

Sears, David O. 1988. "Symbolic Racism." In *Eliminating Racism: Profiles in Controversy*, edited by Phyllis A. Katz and Dalmas A. Taylor, 53–84. New York: Plenum Press.

Segal, Lynne. 1990. *Slow Motion: Changing Masculinities, Changing Men*. London: Virago Press.

Segrest, Mab. 1994. *Memoir of a Race Traitor*. Boston: South End Press.

Sims, Patsy. 1978. *The Klan*. New York: Dorset Press.

Smith, Althea, and Abigail J. Stewart. 1983. "Approaches to Studying Racism and Sexism in Black Women's Lives." *Journal of Social Issues* 39 (3):1–15.

Snitow, Ann, Christine Stansell, and Sharon Thompson, eds. 1983. *Powers of Desire: The Politics of Sexuality*. New York: Monthly Review Press.

Snowden, Frank. 1983. *Before Color Prejudice: The Ancient View of Blacks*. Cambridge, MA: Harvard University Press.

Spelman, Elizabeth V. 1988. *Inessential Woman: Problems in Exclusion in Feminist Thought*. Boston: Beacon Press.

Stanton, Bill. 1991. *Klanwatch: Bringing the Ku Klux Klan to Justice*. New York: Grove Weidenfeld.

Staples, Robert. 1982. *Black Masculinity: The Black Male's Role in American Society*. San Francisco: Black Scholar.

167

————. 1977. "The Myth of the Impotent Black Male." In *The Black Male in America*, edited by Doris Y. Wilkinson and Ronald L. Taylor. Chicago: Nelson-Hall.

————. 1978. "Masculinity and Race: The Dual Dilemma of Black Men." *Journal of Social Issues* 34 (1):169–83.

Stember, Charles Herbert. 1976. *Sexual Racism: The Emotional Barrier to an Integrated Society*. New York: Elsevier.

Theweleit, Klaus. 1987. *Male Fantasies: Women, Floods, Bodies, History*. Translated by Stephen Conway. Minneapolis: University of Minnesota Press.

Thompson, Jerry. 1982. *My Life in the Klan*. New York: Putnam's Sons.

Thompson, John B. 1990. *Ideology and Modern Culture: Critical Social Theory in the Era of Mass Communication*. Stanford, California: Stanford Univeristy Press.

Thornton, Russell. 1987. *American Indian Holocaust and Survival*. Norman, OK: Oklahoma University Press.

Tucker, Richard K. 1991. *The Dragon and the Cross: The Rise and Fall of the Ku Klux Klan in Middle America*. Hamden, CT: Archon Books.

Wade, Wyn Craig. 1987. *The Fiery Cross: The Ku Klux Klan in America*. New York: Simon & Schuster.

Wallace, Michele. 1980. *Black Macho and the Myth of the Superwoman*. New York: Dial.

Ware, Vron. 1992. *Beyond the Pale: White Women, Racism and History*. London: Verson.

Weedon, Chris. 1987. *Feminist Practice and Poststructuralist Theory*. Oxford: Basil Blackwell.

Wellman, David T. 1977. *Portraits of White Racism*. Cambridge: Cambridge University Press.

West, Cornel. 1988. "Marxist Theory and the Specificity of Afro-American Oppression." In *Marxism and the Interpretation of Culture*, edited by Laurence Grossberg, 17–34. Urbana: University of Illinois Press.

White, E. Frances. 1984. "Listening to the Voices of Black Feminism." *Radical America* 18:7–25.

Wilhelm, Sidney M. 1983. *Black in a White America*. Cambridge, MA: Schenkman Publishing.

Wilkinson, Doris Y., and Ronald L. Taylor, eds. 1977. *The Black Male in America: Perspectives on His Status in Contemporary Society*. Chicago: Nelson-Hall.

Woodward, C. Vann. 1974. *The Strange Career of Jim Crow*. New York: Oxford University Press.

Zatarain, Michael. 1990. *David Duke: Evolution of a Klansman*. Gretna, LA: Pelican Publishing.

Index